Dear Anjali & Brent

Thank You for being

my favorite Couple 💜💜

Missing You and wish Your

family a year of Sweetness.

joy and hope ahead!

Merry Christmas With love

Cello

11/15/2020

Raleigh, NC.

Thank You for being
my favorite Couple

Missing you and wish your
family a year of sweetness.
Joy and hope ahead !

Merry Christmas with love
Cello
11/15/2020
Raleigh, No.

FOR THE LOVE OF THE SOUTH

Recipes and Stories from My Southern Kitchen

FOR THE LOVE OF THE SOUTH

Recipes and Stories from My Southern Kitchen

AMBER WILSON

HARPER DESIGN
An Imprint of HarperCollins Publishers

TO MY FAMILY

INTRODUCTION

In the South, the spirit of hospitality—welcoming people into our homes and making them feel loved—is engrained in us. This book goes beyond a love for Southern cuisine and digs deep into the intangibles of the Southern spirit: kindness, warmth, and a love of tradition. I want to share with you memories and meals from a place that is dear to my heart. I hope you feel as though I'm with you in the kitchen, encouraging you as you're stirring roux for gumbo and rolling out pie dough. I hope there are blackberry juice starbursts splattered across the pages, dog-eared corners, and handwritten notes in the margins. Above all, I hope you find comfort in these recipes and make them your own.

I didn't grow up with delicate, handwritten recipe cards that my family members passed down from generation to generation. In fact, I don't remember anyone writing down recipes at all. Instead, I learned by watching the great Southern women before me. Once I had a kitchen of my own, it seemed only natural for me to tie my apron strings and get to work creating my own recipes inspired by the ingredients and dishes I fell in love with. Some recipes use ingredients in ways my grandmothers wouldn't dream of; others hold fast to the integrity of traditional recipes while still pleasing my personal taste. All the recipes have a theme. The ingredients are familiar, simple, economical, and rooted in the region's pantry.

Everything I hold dear about Southern culture rests in its narrative. The photographs throughout this book are personal—as personal as the stories I share. The images of satsuma trees, pecan trees, and cotton crops are taken on family land. Almost all the silver, cast iron, stoneware, and glasses in this book are family treasures. My china pattern and silverware are adorned with one of my favorite flowers, a gardenia, which represents grace and hospitality in the South. The dark wooden background for many photos is an old painter's table discovered at an estate sale in Decatur, Alabama. The marble background is a restored piece from an old home, Rocky Hill, that my husband's family owned. Everything in this book has a story behind it: a meaning, a purpose.

All my memories begin and end with food, and so all my recipes are inspired by memories. It's a mutual relationship. Characters develop around kitchen islands, barbecue pits, and dining room tables. Personalities are interwoven in the strings and strings of meals we've shared, revealing a colorful backdrop for every story I recount. I grew up in a close-knit family. Both sets of grandparents live within ten minutes of each other in Lake Charles, Louisiana. Aunts, uncles, and cousins piled in on the weekends; no one hailed farther than Baton Rouge.

Almost everyone I knew lived in a modest home with enough yard for a satsuma and a fig tree, and a simple garden filled with tomatoes, okra, and peppers. Occasionally, a chicken or pig could be spotted running around backyards, feasting on herbs. We didn't have a lot in the eyes of the world, but we ate like kings—even if our table was littered with crawfish peelings, our throne looked like a broken-in La-Z-Boy recliner, and the crowns we wore denoted our favorite football teams. We *ate* like kings. That's what mattered.

Given the way I grew up surrounded by food, you would think I might have become a chef, food writer, or restaurateur, but the thought never crossed my mind until my senior year of college. In school, I pursued a degree in environmental science and geography. In the first semester of my senior year, I began mulling over topics for my thesis. I wanted to focus on something that interested me, something personal. So, I decided to go in the direction of human geography and chose a nontraditional thesis topic: Southern Food and How Food Defines the South. My professor, a fellow Louisianan, gave her blessing for me to pursue the topic. She recognized my passion for the project and suggested I have coffee with her friend, the editor of a Southern food magazine. While we were having coffee, the editor encouraged me to start a food blog. I simply stated, "I'm not creative. I'm not a professional cook, and I've never picked up a camera. I'm a scientist." Nevertheless, she persuaded me to give it a try, and I did. My site, *For the Love of the South*, became a place where I shared my love for the food, characters, and culture that helped shape who I am. In the meantime, I interviewed to be part of NASA's applied sciences program after graduation. By the time I was offered the position, I had fallen in love with sharing stories and recipes from the South. Looking back, what drew me to science was the prospect of helping preserve everything I loved about my culture, but in a way, that's what I'm doing through food.

This is my story of a region, my home, reduced and boiled down from personal experiences and memories. This book is for the food I can't live without, the region I love, and the people I share my life with. This is for my love of the South.

KITCHEN WISDOM

The kitchen has taught me many things about life, and the greatest guidance I've been given is that preparedness and peace go hand in hand. Preparation and planning help me keep my sanity on days when I'm too busy to cook or too exhausted to stand upright. This is how I cook and live, but at the same time I don't restrict myself to rules or a strict routine, and I don't want you to either. These are suggestions, not orders. Let's be honest, one of the greatest advantages of a home cook's kitchen is that it's one of the only places where complete self-regard is greatly rewarded and guiltlessly pleasurable. This section is full of little pieces of economical and practical kitchen wisdom I've picked up along the way.

STOCKING UP

PANTRY

There's great comfort in knowing my pantry is well stocked. My pantry shelves are lined with spare bags of rice, flour, sugar, a few bags of coffee, boxes of kosher and sea salt, and lots of dried pasta and beans. There is a practical purpose for this. Whenever I am using the last of a kitchen staple in the middle of a recipe, I go to my pantry, knowing I have another bag, box, or bottle waiting for me. Then, I immediately put that item on my shopping list. That way, there are never emergency store runs; just peaceful cooking. The same thinking applies to plastic wrap, parchment paper, paper towels, plastic storage bags, and dish soap. These items are just as important in keeping my kitchen running smoothly and efficiently.

COUNTERTOPS

My countertops reflect changes in both seasons and my mood. Lemons and garlic are displayed year-round in stoneware bowls and silver pedestals. Piles of pears and apples are on the countertop in the fall; satsumas in the winter. During the summer, tomatoes line my countertops and basil plants sit next to my sink in a white vase (in the winter, rosemary takes its place). A copper oil can and a brass pepper mill, along with a small marble condiment bowl filled with kosher salt, sit next to one side of my stove. Glass canisters filled with flour, sugar, and rice are on the other side. I need my kitchen to be functional, but I also need it to be enchanting.

REFRIGERATOR AND FREEZER

I feel empowered every time I open my freezer and refrigerator. At the pull of a handle, I have everything I need to make a meal for my family. There is great comfort in that. My fridge would seem sparse to many people, but I enjoy an organized, clean fridge with everything pushed to the front and condiments with longer expiration dates on the door. Vinaigrettes, greens, and sauces are always in the fridge. During the spring and summer, I keep fresh berries at my fingertips both in the fridge and freezer. As I put away groceries, I tumble berries into a bowl filled with 4 parts cold water and 1 part distilled white vinegar. Swish the berries around and let them sit for 10 minutes. After 10 minutes, drain the vinegar water, rinse the berries well, and drain again. Place the berries in a single layer on a plate lined with a paper towel and keep them in the fridge. I do this for two reasons. This process cleans the berries and it helps them stay lovely and fresh for three to five days, which means your berries will not go bad before you get a chance to enjoy them. Once the berries are fully dried and chilled, I always stash a few fistfuls of berries in quart-size freezer bags and toss them in the freezer so I have frozen berries on hand for recipes like Blackberry Preserves (page 59) and Blackberry Cake (page 232).

I stockpile my freezer with ingredients picked at the height of their season, which is economical since that is when they are at their cheapest, and then I label the bags and freeze them. Along with frozen peach wedges, blackberries, pecans, and whole okra pods, I keep batches of Chili con Carne (page 158), Red Beans and Rice Soup (page 152), and Cajun Chicken and Sausage Gumbo (page 188) for those days I know I won't have time to make a home-cooked meal. (I just move the frozen bags into the fridge to thaw the night before.) Disks of plastic-wrapped pie dough, both sweet and savory, are stashed away in quart-size freezer bags just waiting to be thawed. I always keep boxes of butter in the freezer. Cookie doughs, like the one for my Ginger and Cane Syrup Cookies (page 223), are rolled into logs and kept in the freezer, ready to be sliced, rolled into balls, and baked when I have emergency cookie cravings. My Cane Syrup Caramels (page 211) are tucked away nicely in quart-size freezer bags, waiting to be given away to any unexpected guests. And I have a habit of leaving the base to my ice cream maker in my freezer so I can whip up a batch of ice cream whenever I like.

LABELING

I date and label everything that goes into my fridge, pantry, or freezer. After spending time and money picking out beautiful produce, preparing meals, and carefully storing foods, the worst thing in the world is having to throw away dishes or ingredients because I can't remember how long I've had them. Whenever I spot an ingredient that is on the brink of needing to be tossed, I place it on my countertop along with a cast of characters from the pantry and begin brainstorming about creative ways to prepare the ingredient for dinner. (So many of my favorite meals begin this way.) This habit gives me peace of mind and saves me money hand over fist. I keep a small roll of masking tape along with a black Sharpie in the drawer closest to the fridge to make labeling easy. I even place a little piece of tape on the bottom of my spices with the date to keep an eye on how long they've been in my pantry.

INGREDIENTS

BACON

Bacon demands its own entry. If you've glanced over the recipes yet, you will notice a lot of bacon dishes. And for good reason; I *love* bacon. Sometimes it's the star of the dish, like my Bacon-Latticed Apple Pie (page 238), but most of the time, I use a few slices almost as a seasoning in a dish, adding a smokiness that only bacon can give. Good bacon, especially *really* good bacon, isn't cheap. Here's how I store it so nothing is wasted: grab a gallon-size freezer bag and label it with the date. Cut or fold four or five pieces of parchment or wax paper that are roughly the same size as the plastic bag. Lay the bag flat on your countertop and place the bacon slices in the bag, without touching, in a single layer, then add a piece of the paper over the bacon and continue with another layer. Repeat with the rest of the bacon. Press as much air out of the bag as you can and lay it flat in the freezer. Once the bacon is completely frozen, you can stand it upright. (This is a space saver!) Spending five minutes doing this saves you from worrying about using a whole pound of bacon before it goes bad. If a recipe calls for one or two slices of bacon, just grab the bacon out of the bag and toss it in the skillet frozen. It will fry up beautifully.

DAIRY, FLOUR, AND EGGS

Buttermilk is a staple in the South, therefore it always has a designated spot in my fridge. If you don't have it on hand, don't panic. Simply substitute with whole milk and lemon juice. (One cup of milk to one tablespoon of lemon juice is a good rule of thumb.) Let it sit on the countertop until it thickens, about 5 minutes, before using in a recipe. I only use unsalted butter. Milk is either 2% or whole, and it is always organic. The cream I use is labeled heavy cream or heavy whipping cream. All flours are either all-purpose unbleached white flour or White Lily self-rising flour. Eggs are large and free-range.

GREENS

These have a permanent home in my refrigerator. Whenever I come back from the market, I wash, dry, and store my greens. I pull out my salad spinner and place the spinner in the sink. For delicate lettuces, run cold water down the length of the lettuce leaf. Place the leaves in the salad spinner and spin the leaves until dry. For hearty greens, like kale and collards, fill the salad spinner with cold water. Separate each leaf from the tough central rib of the green by holding the stem in one hand and positioning your thumb and index finger on either side of the base of the leaf. Quickly strip the leaf from the rib in one quick upward motion and place the greens in the spinner. Swish the greens in the cold water and drain. Fill with water again, swish, drain, and repeat the process to triple-wash your greens. You want to remove any grit hiding in the leaves. After you've drained the spinner the third time, spin until the greens are dry. Place the clean lettuce leaves or greens loosely in a plastic storage bag, keeping as much air in the bag as possible. Seal the bag and store in the fridge. Your greens and lettuces will last in the fridge for a week or longer and can be turned into lovely green salads dressed with an elegant vinaigrette, sautéed and baked with eggs, or used in a pasta dish.

OILS

I use four different types of oil: Sunflower oil is my go-to oil for sautéing, pan-frying, and greasing pans and parchment paper. Peanut oil is for deep-frying. Olive oil is for marinades and sauces. Extra-virgin olive oil is used to finish dishes, like pasta and soup, just before serving.

SPICES

I know there are many chefs and home cooks out there who grind their own spices; I'm not one of them. I purchase my spices from a local spice shop that grinds them for me. It's the same price as, if not cheaper than, buying spices at the supermarket, where you have no idea how long they have been sitting there. I do keep a few whole spices on hand, like cinnamon sticks and nutmeg, to finish dishes and drinks.

WATER

Never underestimate the power of water in a recipe. It's pure, doesn't interfere with other flavors in the dish, and it's economical. Many of the dishes I grew up on—gumbos, steamed rice, boils, and soups—always call for water, never stock.

STAPLE BRANDS

There are a few brands that are staples in my pantry. These would be considered specialty items if you don't live in the South, but every ingredient can be found online. I grew up with these ingredients and brands and they remain consistent in quality. They've earned my loyalty. I grew up with chicory coffee and have enjoyed it since I was a little girl. Every morning starts with a steaming cup of chicory café au lait. **Community Coffee** and **French Market** are my favorite brands. **Steen's Cane Syrup** adds a smokiness to sweet dishes that I am addicted to. I use it in place of molasses and syrups. **Zatarain's Creole Mustard** is my mustard of choice. It adds a lovely tanginess to Ravigote Sauce (page 107), vinaigrettes, and homemade mayonnaise (page 149). If I go with any other pepper sauce outside of homemade, it's got to be **Tabasco**. Tabasco's chipotle pepper sauce is my favorite, and you will find it in or accompanying many of my recipes. **Benton's Hickory Smoked Country Bacon** is my bacon of choice. I can find it locally in Nashville, but they also sell it online. If I need self-rising flour for baking, it must be **White Lily**. Cooks in New Orleans swear by **Camellia Brand** red kidney beans for red beans and rice, and so do I. **Cajun Country Rice** is a beautiful rice I stand by; I cook with their long-grain, jasmine, and Toro varieties. Toro rice is the kind my grandmother uses. It is a long-grain rice but has the tenderness of a medium-grain..

CAST IRON

I have an entire cabinet designated for my cast iron collection. Some of the pieces have been passed down from relatives, others were wedding gifts, and the rest I've collected along the way; all are equally cherished. My love for cast iron seems inherited, as these gleaming black skillets were permanent fixtures on the countertops of the kitchens I grew up in. Once I started cooking, it was only natural that I lugged out those same skillets. I quickly began to understand the value of cast iron: It sears meat beautifully, it's essentially nonstick, and once the skillet is hot it stays hot. It's a priceless tool in my kitchen. Don't worry if you don't have an arsenal of cast iron. In many cases, heavy-bottomed pots, nonstick pans, and ovenproof dishes can stand in for cast iron.

One of the most common questions I am asked is how to care for cast iron. Here are a few tips: I use wooden spatulas when I need to continuously scrape the bottom of the cast iron, but I use metal utensils if I am quickly sautéing vegetables or flipping proteins. A well-seasoned skillet—one that is essentially nonstick and has a shiny surface slick from use—can handle acidic foods like tomatoes, but if your skillet is new, acidic foods will strip the seasoning. So, steer clear of vinegar, lemon juice, and tomatoes while you build up your seasoning. After you are finished cooking in your cast iron, allow it to cool slightly and rinse it under hot water. Scrub with a pan brush until clean. Dry the skillet immediately and place it on the stovetop over medium-low heat. While the skillet is heating up, pour a nickel-size drop of flavorless oil, such as sunflower oil, into the skillet. You don't need much! Turn the heat off and rub the oil into the surface of the skillet with a paper towel. Let the skillet cool and dry completely before putting it away.

If you have stubborn residue caked onto your skillet, here's what you do: Place the skillet on medium heat and add water to fill it one-quarter of the way up the side. Once the water begins to boil you will notice the residue releasing from the surface of your skillet. You can use a wooden spatula or spoon to help scrape the bits off the bottom of the skillet. Rinse out the pan. If there is still grime at the bottom, repeat until clean. If necessary, you can use a mild dish soap—but only if it's completely necessary. Just remember to season it afterward.

OTHER COOKING TOOLS

Growing up, we kept our **rice cooker** next to our coffee maker because we used them about the same amount. Rice cookers are a great way to have consistently cooked rice with the flick of a switch. I get lots of use out of my **salad spinner**. In addition to cleaning greens, I also use it to rinse, drain, and dry potatoes for chips and fries. An **ice cream maker** is a must-have to make homemade ice cream at a moment's notice. And there is one appliance that is always on my countertop, partly because it's too heavy to move but mostly because I use it all the time: My **stand mixer** is a permanent fixture in my kitchen. I use it for so many recipes: quickly whipping up egg whites, making homemade mayonnaise and butter, making all sorts of doughs, as well as meringues and cake batters. I even use it to make homemade pasta and sausage with additional attachments. If I'm making small-batch batters or vinaigrettes I reach for my **immersion blender**. I used to say I would never buy a kitchen tool that was designed to make just one thing. Not anymore. My **popover pan** makes me a hypocrite. Popovers in any other pan just don't work for me, but I make popovers enough to justify this pan taking up prime real estate in my cupboard.

PANTRY RECIPES

These are recipes I make often. They are simple and easy to commit to memory. A few dashes of pepper sauce and an elegant vinaigrette elevate dishes with their lovely acidic bite. Steamed rice transforms roasted vegetables or simple soups into a light meal. Homemade vanilla extract and vanilla sugar add a beautiful flavor and depth to sweet breakfasts and desserts.

PEPPER SAUCE

Makes about 1 cup

Homemade pepper sauce sounds fancy, but it's just vinegar infused with chilies. I've always loved the simplicity of pepper sauce and began making it at home with fresh, local chilies. It has the power to brighten dishes that slow-cook for hours like collard greens, gumbos, and stews. Pepper sauce is always served at the table, to be used at each person's pleasure.

Enough Tabasco peppers or Thai chilies to fill an 8-ounce jar
Distilled white vinegar

Pack the whole peppers in an 8-ounce jar and cover with distilled white vinegar. Close tightly. Let the peppers sit in the refrigerator for at least 1 month before using. Keep refrigerated. Decant pepper sauce into a smaller glass cruet or bottle for serving and top off the jar with vinegar one final time to get the most out of your chilies and to always have pepper sauce on hand.

BALSAMIC VINAIGRETTE

Makes about 1⅓ cups

1 cup sunflower oil
⅓ cup balsamic vinegar
1 small garlic clove, finely
  chopped
Pinch of dried oregano
Pinch of sugar
Kosher salt and freshly
  ground black pepper

Put the oil and vinegar in a 2-cup glass measuring cup. Add the garlic, oregano, sugar, and a pinch of salt and pepper. Using an immersion blender, blend for a few seconds until the dressing is thick and creamy. You can also whisk the dressing or shake it in a mason jar. Adjust the sugar, salt, and pepper to taste. Store leftover dressing in the fridge for up to 1 week.

CREOLE MUSTARD VINAIGRETTE

Makes about 1⅓ cups

1 cup sunflower oil
⅓ cup red wine vinegar
2 teaspoons Creole
  mustard
1 small garlic clove, finely
  chopped
Kosher salt and freshly
  ground black pepper

Put the oil and vinegar in a 2-cup glass measuring cup. Add the mustard, garlic, and a pinch of salt and pepper. Using an immersion blender, blend for a few seconds until the dressing is thick and creamy. You can also whisk the dressing or shake it in a mason jar. Adjust the salt and pepper to taste. Store leftover dressing in the fridge for up to 1 week.

STEAMED RICE

Makes about 3 cups

For perfectly steamed rice, I put my trust in my inexpensive four-cup-capacity rice cooker, which is perfect for a batch of gumbo or boudin. Most cookers I've used stand by a 1:1 ratio of rice to water, but you may need to adjust this ratio depending on your cooker.

---

1 cup long-grain rice
1 teaspoon kosher salt

Place the rice in a sieve and rinse under cold water until the water runs clear. Toss the rice into a rice cooker and add 1 cup cold water and the salt. Stir. Place the lid on the rice cooker and cook according to the manufacturer's instructions.

SUPERFINE VANILLA SUGAR

Makes 3 cups

Use this for Vanilla Sugar–Coated Stuffed Doughnuts (page 56), Vanilla-Infused Figs (page 50), or Practically Perfect Popovers (page 136).

---

3 cups granulated sugar
Seeds of 1 vanilla bean

Place the sugar in a food processor and scrape in the vanilla seeds (put the pod in your vanilla extract; recipe follows). Pulse until the vanilla seeds are incorporated into the sugar. Store at room temperature in a large jar.

VANILLA EXTRACT

Makes 2 cups

I started making my own vanilla extract when I realized how quickly I go through the expensive store-bought variety. For that reason, I began buying vanilla beans in bulk—usually once a year. I set aside a few whole beans for recipes using the seeds, but most are used for vanilla extract and vanilla sugar. When you end up with a vanilla bean scraped of its seeds, don't toss it. Place it into your homemade vanilla extract. That way, you are constantly refreshing it. Whenever you run out, simply refill the bottle with vodka and let it sit in the pantry for another 2 to 3 months. If you are an avid baker, or just have a slight obsession with vanilla, you will love having your own little hoard of beans, extract, and vanilla sugar at hand.

---

6 vanilla beans

2 cups vodka

Place the vanilla beans in a clean 1-pint glass jar and top off with vodka. (I use a glass apothecary jar.) Label the bottle with the date and store it in your pantry for 2 to 3 months. After that, you will have lovely, homemade vanilla extract. When properly stored, vanilla extract has an eternal shelf life.

> *Tip:* Once the beans have had a few months to mingle and meld in the vodka, and you have a dark extract, here's one more tip! When a recipe calls for vanilla seeds, you can grab a swollen vanilla pod from the extract and snip one end. Squeeze all the seeds out of the bean like you would squeeze toothpaste out of a tube. Once you've squeezed all the seeds out of the bean, put it back into the vanilla extract.

BREAKFASTS

BROWN BUTTER AND SAGE BAKED EGGS

Serves 1

Brown butter and sage is one of my favorite flavor combinations, and this is a quick, elegant way to take pleasure in these lovely flavors first thing in the morning.

1 tablespoon unsalted
   butter
2 sage leaves
2 eggs, cracked into a
   small bowl
Kosher salt and freshly
   ground black pepper
Sourdough bread, for
   serving

Preheat the oven to 425°F.

Place a small ovenproof skillet over medium-low heat. Place the butter in the skillet, remove from the heat, and swirl it around until it melts. Return the skillet to the heat. After a few minutes, the butter will turn golden and a lovely nutty aroma will fill your kitchen. Take the skillet off the heat and add the sage leaves. Allow the leaves to gently fry for 30 seconds. Add the eggs, transfer the skillet to the oven, and bake until the whites are set and the yolks are still runny, 3 to 5 minutes. Season with salt and pepper.

You can eat the eggs straight from the skillet with a few pieces of bread to soak up all the lovely butter at the bottom of the skillet. (Since the skillet is piping hot, I wrap a tea towel around the handle and the bottom of the skillet before diving in!)

PECAN, FIG, AND GOLDEN RAISIN GRANOLA

Makes about 8 cups

This is a kitchen staple in my house. I always have a stash of granola waiting for me in my fridge, ready to be transferred to a small plastic bag if I am heading out the door on an empty stomach. This granola has every element I desire: vanilla-infused figs and golden raisins, crisp clusters, a hint of cinnamon, and golden honey. If you are using a dark baking sheet, decrease the baking time by 5 to 10 minutes.

1 egg white

½ cup golden raisins

1 cup dried figs, stemmed and roughly chopped

1 tablespoon vanilla extract

Hot water

3 cups old-fashioned rolled oats

1 cup raw pecan halves, roughly chopped

1 cup raw sunflower seeds

2 tablespoons sesame seeds

½ cup packed dark brown sugar

2 teaspoons ground cinnamon

1 teaspoon kosher salt

¼ cup light corn syrup

¼ cup honey

2 tablespoons sunflower oil

Preheat the oven to 325°F. Line a large rimmed baking sheet with parchment paper.

In a stand mixer fitted with a whisk attachment, whip the egg white until stiff peaks form. (You can also use a handheld mixer, or whisk by hand if you are feeling particularly energetic.) Set aside.

In a small bowl, tumble the raisins and figs together. Add the vanilla and enough hot water to barely cover the fruits. This step plumps up the dried fruit so it can stand up to the baking process and will allow the fruit to become part of the coveted granola clusters. Allow the fruit to steep while you prepare the remaining ingredients.

In a large bowl, combine the oats, pecans, sunflower seeds, sesame seeds, brown sugar, cinnamon, and salt. In a small bowl or measuring cup, whisk together the corn syrup, honey, and oil. Pour this over the oat mixture and stir well.

Drain the raisins and figs and toss them into the granola mixture. Stir again. Fold the egg white into the granola. Spread the mixture evenly onto the lined baking sheet. Bake until golden brown, 35 to 40 minutes, rotating the baking sheet halfway through.

Allow the granola to cool on the baking sheet before breaking it up into clusters. Place the cooled granola into a large plastic bag or an airtight container. It will keep in the fridge for weeks.

CARAMELIZED CINNAMON TOAST

Serves 4

My mom always made the best cinnamon toast. I remember how she generously spread the butter onto a piece of hot, perfectly toasted white bread. The butter would melt into a puddle, and a shower of cinnamon sugar would cover the length and breadth of the bread. The sugar would melt on contact in the warmth of the butter. Before I knew it, a pile of cinnamon toast would appear in front of me, and in the blink of an eye, it was gone. All that would remain was a plate of crumbs and the sweet haunting scent of butter and cinnamon.

The morning after my husband, Michael, and I moved into our new loft in Nashville, I began rummaging through kitchen boxes for my toaster to make Mom's cinnamon toast and a coffee maker for my chicory café au lait. All I surfaced with was a kettle, skillet, and French press. Out of desperation for cinnamon toast, I decided to caramelize the toast in a skillet since I couldn't find my toaster. I put the kettle on to boil water for the coffee and stirred together butter, cinnamon, and raw cane sugar, then slathered it on a few slices of bread, and pan-fried it until golden and crispy. I let it cool as I finished making my coffee. This caramelized, crème brûlée–crowned cinnamon toast is the result.

To make the sweet cinnamon butter ahead of time, combine the cinnamon, sugar, and butter and transfer to a sheet of parchment paper. Roll the butter into a log, squeezing and twisting the parchment at both ends like a Christmas cracker. The butter will keep for a week in the fridge.

---

8 tablespoons (1 stick) unsalted butter, at room temperature

3 tablespoons raw cane sugar

1 teaspoon ground cinnamon

8 slices challah, white, or brioche bread

In a small bowl, combine the butter, sugar, and cinnamon.

Place a medium skillet over medium-low heat. While the skillet is preheating, spread one side of each slice of bread with the cinnamon-sugar butter.

Place 4 slices of the buttered bread, butter side down, in the warm skillet. Butter the other side of the bread while the first side toasts. Flip and toast the other side, 1 to 2 minutes per side.

Once both sides are golden and caramelized, transfer to a plate lined with parchment paper. As the toast cools, it will develop a caramelized crème brûlée–like exterior, so the parchment will keep the toast from sticking to the plate. Repeat with the remaining slices of bread and serve.

GRAPEFRUIT WITH YOGURT AND BLACK PEPPER

Serves 1

Whenever I find myself eating alone, I pay close attention to the preparation and presentation of the dish—as much as I would if I were hosting a dinner. You are just as important as any guest you host. I've learned how to celebrate alone time. It's an occasion when I take time carefully segmenting grapefruit. I add just a kiss of honey to the yogurt and dust the grapefruit segments with one twist of my pepper mill. I am usually quick in the kitchen, but when I eat alone, I purposefully slow down. Yogurt with seasonal fruit is my everyday breakfast, along with a glass of juice and a mug (or occasionally a bowl) of chicory coffee laced with sweetened milk. I'm aware that this is hardly a recipe, but it's how I start off nearly every morning. When I'm alone, I gravitate to simple, balanced recipes. Black pepper adds a warmth to fresh citrus, but please feel free to leave it out if you wish. It's one of my favorite flavor combinations.

---

1 large grapefruit, peeled and segmented
⅓ cup plain yogurt
1 tablespoon honey
Freshly ground black pepper

Arrange the grapefruit wedges on one side of a plate.

In a small bowl, mix together the yogurt and honey and spoon the sweetened yogurt next to the grapefruit. Lightly season the grapefruit with black pepper.

HOW TO EAT ALONE

A patron of the restaurant I worked at came every Saturday morning at precisely eleven o'clock. He was short, thin, and elderly, dressed in perfectly creased tweed slacks and a crisp button-down shirt. He always had a Waco, Texas, newspaper tucked under his right arm. Wrinkles around his eyes and cheeks folded gently into one another as he greeted me. His wide, toothy smile was stained from a lifetime of daily indulgences: drinking coffee and red wine, and smoking cigarettes. We walked through the restaurant to his favorite table, number 26. The small, circular bistro table was the second to last in a row of identical tables in the atrium. The atrium was long and narrow. Small windowpanes stretched from the floor to the curved ceiling, which poured sunshine into the otherwise dark restaurant. I sat with him for just a few minutes before having to dash away as the lunch crowd began to pick up.

He would sit at table number 26 for nearly two hours. He ordered a glass of red wine to drink with his appetizer; he ordered another glass of wine with his entrée. As he enjoyed his meal, he would alternate between people-watching and reading his newspaper, spectacles balancing dangerously close to the end of his nose. He sat with his right leg draped over his left. His foot bounced in the air every few seconds, drawing attention to his shiny doll-like shoes. For dessert he drank coffee, which arrived with a small silver cup of cold cream, and he ate milk chocolate cake sitting on top of a pool of dark chocolate ganache scattered with berries. By this time, the lunch crowd usually had come and gone, and I was able to sit with him again as he enjoyed his dessert.

For many months, I was curious about why he never invited anyone to eat with him at his favorite restaurant at table number 26. He told me he was a widower, but his children and grandchildren lived in town. After a few months passed, the answer became clear.

Most people are embarrassed to eat alone or try to avoid it completely. He dined alone intentionally and savored every second. Silently and unknowingly, he taught me a great lesson: how to eat alone and enjoy the company.

A MESS OF EGGS AND KALE

Serves 1

I love how kale chars and gets crispy in this dish. This is a lovely breakfast but also makes an excellent lunch when served between two slices of sourdough toast slathered with Chipotle Mayonnaise (page 142).

Olive oil
½ bunch kale, tough ribs
    removed, triple-washed
    (page 18)
Pinch of red pepper flakes
Kosher salt and freshly
    ground black pepper
2 eggs, cracked into a
    small bowl
Tabasco chipotle pepper
    sauce
Lemon wedge

Preheat the oven to 425°F.

Coat a medium skillet with olive oil and set over medium heat. Once the oil is hot, add the kale, red pepper flakes, and salt and black pepper to taste. (The kale will spit from any moisture clinging to the leaves.) Toss the kale until bright green and charred in a few places, 1 to 2 minutes.

Remove the skillet from the heat and carefully slide the eggs onto the top of the sautéed kale. Transfer the skillet to the oven and bake until the whites are set but the yolks are still runny, about 8 minutes. Lightly season the eggs with salt, pepper, and chipotle pepper sauce. Transfer the greens and eggs to a plate and spritz with a few drops of lemon juice just before serving.

VARIATION

Eggs with Turnip or Collard Greens: This recipe is delicious with turnip or collard greens, too. Simply substitute ½ bunch greens for the kale. (Remove the tough stems and triple-wash the greens.) If you want the dish to be a little spicier, substitute a pinch of cayenne pepper for the red pepper flakes. If you prefer a classic, vinegary hum to your greens, swap a small drizzle of Pepper Sauce (page 25) for the Tabasco chipotle pepper sauce.

MUSCADINE DUTCH BABY

Serves 2

Muscadines are a lovely summertime treat in the South. The skin of a muscadine is much thicker than other grapes, and the skin bursts and separates from the pale green flesh as you bite into it. The flesh is sweet and juicy, and the skin is tart. The seeds from the muscadine are vibrant green, the size of a sunflower kernel, and wonderfully bitter and slightly sour at the same time. It's a divine combination. If I don't have fresh fruit on hand, I simply spritz the Dutch baby with lemon juice and dust it with powdered sugar.

This is one of my favorite breakfasts because I can make the batter the night before, which eliminates the need to measure anything before I've had my morning coffee; and it never fails to impress as the effortless puffy pancake comes out of the oven. I like to serve tart fruit with a Dutch baby to balance out the sweetness of the dish: Muscadines, blackberries, and dark cherries are a few of my favorites. To make the batter ahead of time, just cover the batter tightly once it's blended up and stash it away in the fridge overnight. Though it is not necessary to rest the batter, I find it creates a lovely, ruffled Dutch baby.

¼ cup all-purpose flour

¼ cup milk

2 large eggs

2 tablespoons granulated sugar

2 teaspoons vanilla extract

Pinch of kosher salt

1 tablespoon unsalted butter, at room temperature

1 handful of muscadines, halved and seeded

Powdered sugar, for dusting

Place a medium ovenproof skillet in the oven and preheat to 425°F.

In a blender, combine the flour, milk, eggs, granulated sugar, vanilla, and salt and blend until smooth. (Alternatively, combine the ingredients in a bowl and blend with an immersion blender or whisk for a few minutes until completely smooth.)

Remove the preheated pan from the oven, add the butter, and swirl it around until it melts. Brush the melted butter up the sides of the skillet. Pour the batter into the skillet and immediately return to the oven. Bake until the edges are golden and puffy, 15 to 20 minutes. Arrange the muscadines on top and dust with powdered sugar. Cut in half and serve.

VARIATION

Almond and Cherry Dutch Baby: Replace the vanilla extract with ¼ teaspoon almond extract and bake as directed. Finish the Dutch baby with 1 cup halved pitted cherries.

PAW-PAW'S PAIN PERDU WITH VANILLA-INFUSED FIGS

Serves 4

My grandfather, Paw-Paw, made *pain perdu* (French toast) for my sister and me whenever we spent the night at our grandparents' house. It was always perfect: crisp on the outside and custardy on the inside. *Pain perdu* literally means "lost bread" in French. It's a delicious and economical way to make use of bread that is stale or "lost." Challah is my favorite bread for *pain perdu*, but you can also use day-old baguette, brioche, or white sandwich bread. This is an assembly-line recipe: Once one batch comes out of the skillet, another batch will be ready to go in.

½ cup whole milk

3 large eggs

⅓ cup packed dark brown sugar

2 tablespoons honey

2 tablespoons vanilla extract

1 teaspoon ground cinnamon

Pinch of kosher salt

8 slices challah bread (½- to 1-inch thick)

Sunflower oil

Powdered sugar

Vanilla-Infused Figs (following page)

Set an ovenproof serving plate in the oven and preheat to the lowest possible setting.

In a shallow dish, whisk together the milk, eggs, brown sugar, honey, vanilla, cinnamon, and salt. Dip two slices of bread into the custard.

Place a medium skillet over medium heat. Coat the bottom of the skillet with oil.

Once the custard begins to soak through the bread, flip it. Allow the flipside to soak in the custard for 1 to 2 minutes. Place both slices of custard-soaked bread into the preheated skillet. Immediately place two more slices of bread into the custard to soak.

Once the bread is deeply golden on one side, flip and cook the other side. Flip the slices that are soaking in the custard too. Reduce the heat if you notice the bread browning too quickly.

Place the cooked *pain perdu* onto the preheated serving plate and return it to the oven. This will keep the bread warm while you finish frying the remaining slices.

Pour a little more oil in the skillet and repeat the process of soaking and cooking the bread slices until all are golden.

Once all the bread slices are cooked, remove the plate from the oven and dust with powdered sugar. Serve the *pain perdu* with the Vanilla-Infused Figs.

VANILLA-INFUSED FIGS

Makes about 3 cups

In addition to Paw-Paw's Pain Perdu, you can serve these delicious figs spooned over a Dutch Baby (page 46), with yogurt, or on top of ice cream.

¼ cup **Superfine Vanilla Sugar (page 28)**
¼ cup **raw cane sugar**
2 cups **hot water**
1 tablespoon **lemon juice**
Pinch of **ground cinnamon**
Pinch of **kosher salt**
1 pound **fresh figs, stems pinched off**

In a small saucepan, combine the vanilla sugar, cane sugar, water, lemon juice, cinnamon, and salt. Bring to a gentle boil over medium heat, then reduce the heat to low. As soon as the syrup settles to a simmer, add the figs and partially cover with the lid. The syrup will be quite thin and light. Simmer the figs in syrup for 30 minutes. The figs will puff up like balloons as they simmer. Gently stir the figs occasionally, being careful not to pop the delicate skins.

AMBROSIA FRUIT SALAD

Serves 2 to 4

I remember the first time I encountered ambrosia salad. I was around five years old and desperate for a snack. As I began shuffling through my grandmother's fridge, I noticed a clear glass bowl filled with what looked and smelled like lime green Jell-O and Cool Whip. Pecans, citrus segments, coconut flakes, and marshmallows were suspended throughout. I grabbed a spoon and cautiously carved a bit of the salad out of the bowl. It tasted of every element I observed in the bowl. Nothing more, nothing less. What confused me most about this salad was how it was served alongside the main course, as if it was a normal green salad! (It seemed like something that should be served at the breakfast table.) My ambrosia salad has most of the elements of the old-fashioned classic just presented in a new way. Coconut-flavored yogurt pairs well with the citrus and pomegranate, and it is a nod to the traditional flavors in ambrosia. This salad tastes best whenever citrus are at their peak; but if you want to make this salad any time of year, use regular oranges in place of the satsumas and the blood oranges. I love serving ambrosia salad alongside eggs, bacon, and coffee for a lovely brunch for four or divide between two bowls for a light breakfast!

1½ cups coconut, vanilla, or plain yogurt

2 large grapefruits, peeled and segmented, with membranes removed

3 medium blood oranges, peeled and segmented, with membranes removed

3 small satsumas, peeled and cut crosswise into ¼-inch-thick rounds

½ large pomegranate

Spread the yogurt into a shallow, rimmed serving dish. Scatter the grapefruit segments, blood orange segments, and satsuma rounds over the yogurt. With a large spoon in one hand and a pomegranate half in the other, whack the back of the pomegranate and let the seeds fall onto the salad. Make sure you squeeze the pomegranate half, letting the juice dress the citrus.

BAKED EGGS WITH CRISPY GREEN ONIONS

Serves 1

I opened my fridge one day desperate for a light breakfast—no carbs, no butter, just a delicious egg dish—and I needed to use leftover green onions that were staring at me. This recipe is the result, and it's become one of my go-to dishes when I need a quick, healthy, yet still comforting, breakfast. Cooking green onions in a dry pan brings out the sweetness in the onion, and makes them incredibly crisp and irresistible.

2 green onions (scallions), white and pale green parts only

2 teaspoons sunflower oil

2 eggs, cracked into a small bowl

Kosher salt and freshly ground black pepper

Preheat the oven to 425°F.

Halve the green onions lengthwise and then crosswise.

Place a small ovenproof skillet over medium heat. Once the skillet is hot, arrange the onions in a single layer. Gently press down on the onions with the back of a fork and brown on both sides. This will only take 1 to 2 minutes.

Remove the skillet from the heat and add the oil. Gently move the green onions around, making sure the oil coats the bottom of the skillet as well as underneath the onions. Add the eggs, transfer the skillet to the oven, and bake until the whites are set but the yolk is still runny, 5 to 7 minutes. Season with salt and pepper and eat straight from the skillet!

VANILLA SUGAR–COATED STUFFED DOUGHNUTS

Makes 12 doughnuts

When I first made Justin Gellatly's doughnut recipe (from St. John Bakery in London), I was reminded of the doughnuts I grew up eating on Saturday mornings. I've adapted his recipe slightly and have included the recipes for my favorite doughnut fillings: Blackberry Preserves, Sea Salt Caramel Cream, Grapefruit Curd, and Satsuma Marmalade. Since this dough rests overnight in the fridge and again at room temperature for 2 to 3 hours, I save this recipe for lazy weekend brunches.

---

2 cups all-purpose flour, plus more for dusting

3 tablespoons sugar

1 teaspoon kosher salt

1½ teaspoons rapid rise (fast-acting) yeast

2 large eggs, at room temperature

2 teaspoons grated lemon zest

¼ cup plus 2 tablespoons warm water

4 tablespoons unsalted butter, at room temperature

Sunflower oil, for greasing

Peanut oil, for frying

Superfine Vanilla Sugar (page 28), for coating

In a stand mixer fitted with a flat beater attachment, combine the flour, sugar, salt, yeast, eggs, lemon zest, and water. Beat on medium speed until the dough begins to pull away from the sides of the bowl and form a ball, about 8 minutes. Let the dough rest for 1 minute.

Continue mixing on medium speed and slowly add the butter, about 1 teaspoon at a time. Once the butter is incorporated, mix on high until the dough is glossy, smooth, and elastic, about 5 minutes.

Lightly grease a medium bowl with sunflower oil. Scoop the dough into the bowl, cover lightly with plastic wrap, and let it rise until doubled in size, 1 to 1½ hours. Quickly knead the dough in the bowl to let the air out and tightly re-cover. Chill overnight or up to 24 hours.

Line a large rimmed baking sheet with parchment paper and dust with flour. Lightly flour a work surface and cut the dough into 12 equal pieces. Roll each piece of dough into a tight ball, either by rolling the dough between your palms or on the work surface. Place on the prepared baking

2 cups Blackberry Preserves (page 59), Sea Salt Caramel Cream (page 60), Grapefruit Curd (page 61), or Satsuma Marmalade (page 62), for filling

sheet and sprinkle more flour on the tops of the dough. Cover lightly with plastic wrap and let the dough rise until doubled in size, 2 to 3 hours.

In a heavy-bottomed medium pot, heat 2 to 3 inches of peanut oil over medium heat to 360°F. Line a plate with paper towels. Once the oil preheats, gently pick up a ball of dough and carefully slide the dough into the oil. Place 2 more balls of dough into the oil and set a timer for 2 minutes. Gently flip the doughnuts and fry on the other side for an additional 2 minutes. Drain on the prepared plate for a minute or so. Toss the hot fried doughnuts into a shallow dish with the vanilla sugar. Stand the doughnuts up in a deep baking dish.

Repeat to fry the remaining dough in batches of three. Don't forget to keep an eye on the thermometer, making sure the temperature of the oil stays at 360°F. Adjust the heat as needed as you are frying the doughnuts.

Once the doughnuts have cooled slightly, pierce the "seam" of the doughnut with a paring knife, creating a pocket for the filling. Use your finger to coax a wider opening for the filling. Spoon your filling of choice into a gallon-size plastic bag. Gather the filling to one corner of the bag and twist it, creating your own pastry bag. Cut the tip off the bag and generously fill each doughnut.

Serve the doughnuts standing up to reveal the blackberry, caramel cream, grapefruit curd, or satsuma filling. For the blackberry filling, I cap each doughnut with a fresh blackberry. Devour immediately.

BLACKBERRY PRESERVES

Makes 2 cups

You can make these preserves a week ahead and store them in the fridge until you are ready to fill the doughnuts. Just make sure to take the preserves out of the fridge while the balls of dough rest. If you use frozen blackberries, there is no need to thaw them. These preserves are also lovely served with Sugar and Spice Popovers (page 137).

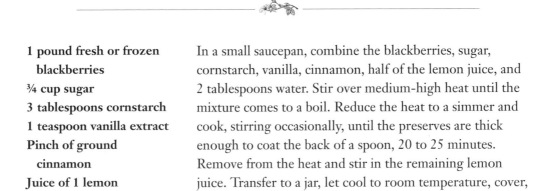

1 pound fresh or frozen blackberries

¾ cup sugar

3 tablespoons cornstarch

1 teaspoon vanilla extract

Pinch of ground cinnamon

Juice of 1 lemon

In a small saucepan, combine the blackberries, sugar, cornstarch, vanilla, cinnamon, half of the lemon juice, and 2 tablespoons water. Stir over medium-high heat until the mixture comes to a boil. Reduce the heat to a simmer and cook, stirring occasionally, until the preserves are thick enough to coat the back of a spoon, 20 to 25 minutes. Remove from the heat and stir in the remaining lemon juice. Transfer to a jar, let cool to room temperature, cover, and refrigerate until ready to use.

SEA SALT CARAMEL CREAM

Makes 2 cups

Before filling the doughnuts with this cream, the insides need to be close to room temperature. (The filling will begin to melt if the doughnuts are too hot.) Any leftover filling can be stashed away in the fridge for up to a week to dollop on pancakes, waffles, a Muscadine Dutch Baby (page 46), or Paw-Paw's Pain Perdu (page 49).

¼ cup sugar

2 tablespoons unsalted butter

2 tablespoons plus 1 cup heavy (whipping) cream

½ teaspoon cane syrup

¾ teaspoon vanilla extract

Pinch of sea salt

MAKE THE SEA SALT CARAMEL:

In a small saucepan, combine the sugar and 1 tablespoon water over low heat. Once the sugar completely dissolves, add the butter and bring to a boil. Keep an eye on the pot! When the liquid turns amber in color, remove from the heat and add 2 tablespoons of the cream, the cane syrup, vanilla, and salt. It will bubble up and steam a lot so stand back. Keep stirring until smooth. Transfer to a small jar, cover, and let cool in the fridge for a few hours or overnight.

MAKE THE CARAMEL CREAM:

In a bowl, whisk the remaining 1 cup cream until stiff peaks form. Whisk the cold caramel into the cream. Store in the fridge until you are ready to fill the cooled doughnuts.

GRAPEFRUIT CURD

Makes 2 ⅔ cups

The slight bitterness of the grapefruit juice cuts the sweetness and richness of this curd in a beautiful way. Any leftover curd can be stashed in the fridge for up to one week. Slather the curd onto toast or fold into vanilla yogurt for breakfast.

½ cup cornstarch

1 cup granulated sugar

½ cup raw cane sugar

1¼ cups grapefruit juice (from about 1½ grapefruits)

Juice of 1 lemon

¼ teaspoon kosher salt

4 large egg yolks, at room temperature

4 tablespoons unsalted butter, at room temperature

In a medium saucepan, combine the cornstarch, granulated sugar, cane sugar, grapefruit juice, lemon juice, salt, and ½ cup water. Whisk over medium-high heat until all the ingredients are combined and the mixture comes to a boil. Let boil for 1 minute, until thick and pale pink in color. Take off the heat.

In a small bowl, whisk the egg yolks. Slowly whisk the grapefruit mixture into the yolks. Return the filling to the saucepan and cook over low heat, whisking constantly for 1 minute more. Do not let the mixture come to a boil.

Remove the pan from the heat and whisk in the butter, a bit at a time, until all the butter is incorporated. Pour the filling into a small container and cover the surface with plastic wrap. This will keep your filling from getting a skin on the top as it cools. Allow the filling to cool for 1 to 2 hours in the fridge before filling the doughnuts.

SATSUMA MARMALADE

Makes ten to twelve 4-ounce jars

Satsuma marmalade is one of my favorite preserves. The thin, delicate skin of a satsuma is thinner than an orange and the juice is a little sweeter as well, so it makes for a beautiful, well-balanced marmalade. This recipe does take some time, but one batch of this marmalade will get me through to the next satsuma season, so it's worth the extra effort. You can use half-pint jars, but I prefer smaller jars of marmalade, which I keep in my pantry and give away as gifts. It's important to buy organic satsumas and lemons and to thoroughly rinse the skin before using.

---

16 satsumas, unpeeled, quartered into wedges, then cut into ¼-inch-thick slices (about 8 cups)

Grated zest and juice of 1 lemon

Seeds of 1 vanilla bean

8 cups sugar

In a large, heavy-bottomed, nonreactive pot, combine the satsumas, lemon zest, lemon juice, and 8 cups cold water. Bring to a boil over high heat, then remove from the heat. Stir in the vanilla seeds and sugar, and keep stirring until the sugar dissolves. Cover the pot and let it sit at room temperature for at least 3 hours or preferably overnight.

Bring the cooled mixture to a boil, then place the lid slightly askew and simmer over low heat for 2 hours. Increase the heat to medium and gently boil for 30 minutes, stirring often. (This step may take closer to 45 minutes if you have an induction range.) Cook until the marmalade reaches 220°F.

Meanwhile, fill a stockpot three-quarters of the way up with water and bring to a boil. Once the water comes to a boil, use tongs to carefully lower in clean jars, rings, and seals. Make sure everything is covered with water and boil for 20 minutes. Turn off the heat, cover, and keep the jars in the warm water until you are ready to fill them. After you have sterilized the jars, line a medium pot with a clean white towel. Fill the pot three-quarters of the way up with water and bring to a gentle boil. (This pot of boiling water will be used to process the jars once they are filled.)

Use tongs to carefully remove the sterilized jars, rings, and seals from the water bath, and ladle the marmalade into the jars, leaving ¾ to 1 inch of space at the top. Wipe the rims with a clean cloth and place the seals carefully on the jars. Twist the rings onto the jars just until fingertip tight. Use tongs to place the jars in the pot of gently boiling water lined with a towel, making sure the jars are covered by at least 1 inch of water. Allow the jars to boil for 10 minutes.

Cool completely on the countertop for 24 hours before storing. You should hear a symphony of popping sounds as the jars seal. Test the jars' seal by pressing the middle of each lid. If there is no give, the jars are ready to be stashed away safely in the pantry for up to a year. If the middle of the lid pops back when pressed, the jar did not seal properly. Stash any improperly sealed jars in the fridge and use within one week.

SATSUMA KISSES

Glistening jars of jams and jellies regularly adorn my breakfast table. Satsuma marmalade reminds me of melted glass jewels ready to be slathered onto piping hot cornbread, popovers, or toast. Satsumas are especially lovely citrus to preserve because of their wonderful sweetness and delicate skin. Vanilla seeds add warmth and depth to the marmalade. The scent of citrus and vanilla takes me back to winter mornings in my grandmother's backyard in Lake Charles, Louisiana.

There is a plentiful satsuma tree in the center of her yard, and an old post where a white wooden swing used to be. Its worn and weathered body has since collapsed, but I remember, when I was about five, walking to the swing after gathering about ten or so satsumas in the bottom of my shirt. I sat there alone, swinging as I pierced the thin reddish orange peel from the satsuma with my thumbnail. Carefully, I removed the spongy strings that held the plump fruit to its shell. I sectioned out the segments, setting aside the "kiss" (a tiny sliver nestled in between two other satsuma slices), and, one by one, I popped the sweet morsels in my mouth. The satsuma burst as I bit into it, and the sweet clear juice exploded from the swollen segment. I placed the "kisses" in a white napkin and shoved them into the right front pocket of my jeans for safekeeping. Satsuma "kisses" are meant to be shared with those you love. One by one, I handed tiny "kisses" to family members, letting them know just how much I loved them.

Back in my kitchen in Nashville, the heat of the range and my morning cup of chicory coffee keep me warm as I stir the simmering marmalade. *Blip, blip, blip* . . . The scent of sugar and citrus wafts through the house. One by one, the crystal clear quilted jars fill with sunny, warm marmalade flecked with vanilla seeds. There is comfort in my heart and stomach knowing I can make my beloved satsuma season last for the rest of the year. Having these little jars of jewels is like having a cool taste of winter during summer's heat. As soon as I twist off the lid of the quilted glass jar, I recall my grandmother's yard. Sitting at my breakfast table only inches away from my fingertips in that gleaming jar is a piece of home.

DRINKS
&
APPETIZERS

GEORGIA PEACH BELLINI

Makes 6 drinks

One peach per drink is a good rule of thumb to keep in mind, especially if you are making this drink for a crowd. If you want to make a batch for the kids, simply substitute sparkling water for prosecco. You may need to allow the peaches to sit on the countertop a few days to ripen perfectly for this recipe. The peaches should smell heavenly and be soft when the skin is pressed.

---

6 ripe peaches, rinsed
1 (750-ml) bottle of prosecco or sparkling water

Place a fine-mesh sieve over a glass measuring cup or bowl with a spout for easy pouring. One by one, squeeze the peaches over the sieve, rubbing the flesh and skin against the mesh. (Rubbing the skin against the mesh gives the peach puree its lovely color.) Discard the pits and skin. Repeat until you've "hand pureed" all the peaches.

Add 1 cup of prosecco to the puree, stir, and divide this mixture among six highball glasses, topping off the glasses with more prosecco. Enjoy!

VARIATION

Strawberry Bellini: Strawberries make for a beautiful summertime Bellini. Place 1 sprig of mint between your palms and slap your hands together. This may seem like a funny thing to do, but you are activating the oils in the mint. Place the mint at the bottom of a sieve set over a 2-cup measuring cup. Toss 2 cups hulled strawberries into the sieve and push them against the mesh with the back of a spoon to extract the juice. Discard the solids. Add 1 cup prosecco to the strawberry puree, stir, and divide the mixture among highball glasses. Top off with more prosecco.

LOUISIANA PECAN, HONEY, AND SEA SALT MILK

Makes 4 drinks

Pecan milk is like bottling up and drinking the essence of the Louisiana pecans that my grandfather lovingly cared for. Find the freshest pecans you can for this recipe. You can reuse the leftover strained pecan meal in several ways: I add some of the damp meal to cornbread batter or pancake batter. It's also yummy stirred into oatmeal. You can add it to a vanilla ice cream base to make pecan ice cream!

---

1 cup pecan halves
2 tablespoons honey
Pinch of sea salt
4 cups hot filtered water

Place the pecans in a medium bowl and add water to cover by 2 inches. Let them soak for at least 12 hours. The longer the pecans soak, the creamier and smoother the milk will be.

Drain the pecans (discard the soaking liquid). In a blender, combine the pecans, honey, salt, and filtered water and blend on low speed, increasing the speed to high for at least 2 minutes.

Strain the pecan milk through a tea towel or a fine-mesh sieve into a medium bowl, pressing down on the solids (discard or reuse the pecan meal). Adjust the sweetness and saltiness of the milk.

THE PECAN TREES

Outlined against the illuminating midwinter sky, delicate branches of our pecan trees gently wave like aging hands toward heaven as if in prayer. Emerald fruits the size of a newborn's fist are scattered under the bowing boughs of the ancient trees. Green husks of the pecan fruits peel away in damp shards, revealing the black and brown tiger-striped shells.

My grandfather is the most patient man I have ever met, and, therefore, the perfect caretaker of the pecan trees. Branches are carefully pruned back with his trusty shears. The leaves of the tree are kept under close surveillance, and any sign of disease is immediately treated. He carefully wraps chicken wire around the trunks, which protects the bark from being stripped by pesky critters. He is tender at heart, wrinkled around the eyes, and deeply grounded. After gathering pecans, he perches himself at the kitchen table, his mighty, weathered hands grasping the pewter nutcracker. The weight of the metal jaws breaks the shell, exposing the tender meat of the pecan. Meticulously separating the two halves from the center of the nut, he places the pecans in clear plastic bags simply labeled with the date. There are the occasional broken stragglers that *must* be tasted for quality control. It's a sweet reward for collecting the beloved pecans.

Some years the trees are barren, either from drought or an autumn storm, which strips the trees of their green fruit. But, then, the following year they are fertile once again. My granddad is patient and tends the pecan trees, like a member of the family in need of loving care.

SATSUMA MIMOSAS

Makes 2 drinks

At the first grown-up Christmas party I ever attended, mimosas were passed around to the adults on silver trays. As a young girl, I remember dreaming of being older and drinking mimosas out of a coupe champagne glass. Now that I'm older, I do.

This is hardly a recipe, but I adore the sweeter flavor of satsuma juice over orange in this simple, classic drink. During the winter, when satsumas are in season, I buy as many as I can and juice them. I strain the juice, transfer it to quart freezer bags, lay the bags flat until frozen solid, then stack the frozen juice side by side like library books in my freezer. This way, I can have satsuma mimosas year-round! If you are using frozen juice instead of fresh, keep in mind that the ratio for a mimosa is equal parts champagne to juice.

Juice of 1 medium satsuma, strained

Champagne or prosecco

Divide the juice between two champagne glasses and top with your favorite champagne or prosecco for a lovely, effortless drink!

FRUIT TEA PUNCH

Makes 12 drinks

Fruit tea is a Nashville staple. The original recipe does not contain alcohol, but the addition of booze makes it the perfect crowd-pleasing punch for a party (I've also included a variation of Fruit Tea Punch for two cocktails). If you want to serve a nonalcoholic version of this recipe, simply substitute water for vodka.

For the Sweet Tea Simple Syrup:
1 cup boiling water
1 cup sugar
2 family-size black tea bags (or 3 regular-size bags)

For the Fruit Tea Punch:
2 cups vodka
2 cups fresh pineapple juice
2 cups fresh orange juice
½ cup fresh lemon juice
½ cup fresh lime juice
Ice, for serving

MAKE A SWEET TEA SIMPLE SYRUP:

Pour boiling water into a glass measuring cup and add the sugar. Stir until the sugar dissolves completely. Add the tea bags and steep for 5 minutes, stirring occasionally. Discard the tea bags. Cover and chill the syrup until ready to use. This syrup can be made up to a week in advance.

MAKE THE FRUIT TEA PUNCH:

Pour the Sweet Tea Simple Syrup, vodka, pineapple juice, and citrus juices into a punch bowl and stir. Fill the bowl with ice and serve with a ladle.

VARIATION

Fruit Tea Punch Cocktail: Combine ¼ cup vodka, ¼ cup fresh pineapple juice, ¼ cup fresh orange juice, 1 tablespoon each fresh lemon and lime juices, and 3 tablespoons of Sweet Tea Simple Syrup in an ice-filled cocktail shaker (or a jar with a lid). Shake for a few seconds and divide between two ice-filled old-fashioned glasses.

A BIN WITH A VIEW

Louisiana summer feasts were never complete without a sweet, refreshing slice of cantaloupe. I recall my mother teaching me how to pick out the perfectly ripe melon for dinner at our local grocery store, Market Basket, in Lake Charles. I crawled out from under the basket, stood on the edge of the cart, and reached over into the cantaloupe bin. The tiny treasures in my overalls started to fall out of my pockets and onto the red and black checkered floor. I glanced at my mom for a little help, and she held me by the side so I could have a better view of the cantaloupe bin.

My mom explained how I needed to look for a melon with little to no markings, bruises, or scars. She told me to knock on the melon with my fist. I didn't quite understand the importance of this action, but I took the advantage of thumping the cantaloupe twice while saying, "Knock, knock, is anybody home?" The next step was by far the most important and the most wonderful.

I took the melon with both hands and slowly cradled it next to my nose, closed my eyes, and took a deep breath. The smell of sugar and earth filled my nostrils and without hesitation I looked up at my mom and said, "This one is ready!" And there I sat, underneath the cart, with my cantaloupe in one hand and the other hand resting under my head, thinking and dreaming of dinner and the sweet taste of perfectly ripe cantaloupe.

CANTALOUPE LEMONADE

Makes about 4½ cups

I can't think of a more refreshing, effortless way to serve cantaloupe than with this cantaloupe lemonade. The sweetness of the melon complements the tart lemonade in a beautiful way. Leftover cantaloupe can be sliced, covered, and stashed away in the fridge for later. For an elegant summertime cocktail, top off cantaloupe lemonade with prosecco or sparkling wine.

½ cup cantaloupe juice (see Tip)
½ cup fresh lemon juice (from about 1½ lemons)
½ cup sugar
½ cup boiling water
Ice, for serving

Add the cantaloupe juice to a large pitcher along with the lemon juice and 3 cups cold water.

In a bowl, stir together the sugar and boiling water until the sugar dissolves completely. Pour the syrup into the pitcher and stir for a few seconds. Serve over ice!

Tip: To make the cantaloupe juice, roughly chop ¼ of a peeled medium cantaloupe. Puree the cantaloupe using a blender or an immersion blender and strain the cantaloupe puree through a fine-mesh sieve.

MILK PUNCH

Makes 1 drink

This New Orleans cocktail is as classic as a Sazerac. It's a lovely cocktail to serve, especially around the holidays, as this boozy, not too sweet, creamy cocktail is the South's answer to eggnog. This cocktail is traditionally served at brunch after a night of overindulgence in New Orleans.

½ ounce Simple Syrup (recipe follows)

1 ounce spiced rum

1 ounce heavy (whipping) cream

1 ounce whole milk

Freshly grated nutmeg, for garnish

In an ice-filled cocktail shaker (or glass jar), combine the Simple Syrup, rum, cream, and milk and shake for 1 minute until frothy. Strain into a champagne coupe (or any other small cocktail glass). Garnish with grated nutmeg.

SIMPLE SYRUP

Makes ¾ cup

½ cup boiling water

½ cup granulated sugar

Pour the boiling water over the granulated sugar in a 2-cup measuring cup. Stir until the sugar completely dissolves. Store in the fridge until ready to use or for up to 1 week.

FRENCH 77

Makes 1 drink

This is a variation of a French 75. Story has it the original cocktail, which is made of cognac or gin, champagne, lemon, and sugar, packed a kick like a French 75-mm field gun. I love the floral notes the elderflower liqueur adds to this cocktail. I usually leave out the stronger spirits, making this a light version.

½ ounce elderflower
    liqueur
¼ ounce fresh lemon juice
¼ ounce Simple Syrup
    (page 82)
Champagne
Lemon peel, for garnish

In an ice-filled cocktail shaker, combine the elderflower liqueur, lemon juice, and Simple Syrup. Shake well. Strain into a champagne glass, top off with champagne, and garnish with the lemon peel.

VARIATION

Classic French 75: Substitute 1¼ ounces cognac or gin for the elderflower liqueur.

CHICORY CAFÉ AU LAIT

Makes 1 drink

I drink this café au lait every morning. It's half sweetened milk and half chicory coffee, which I serve in a warmed small bowl or large mug. I have an inexpensive handheld milk frother that I use to dissolve the sugar in the warm milk while frothing it at the same time. If you don't have a frother, no worries, just stir the sugar in the milk with a spoon.

½ cup 2% or whole milk

Raw cane sugar

½ cup brewed chicory coffee (or other favorite coffee or espresso)

In a small butter warmer or saucepan, warm the milk over low heat until steaming, then add sugar to taste. Stir or froth together until the sugar completely dissolves.

Pour the coffee into a café au lait bowl or large mug. Top with the sweetened milk.

CHICORY COFFEE AND RITUALS

I remember drinking my very first cup of chicory coffee at the age of three. I stretched out my hands and took hold of the cold crystal glass Grannie set in front of me. My fingernails slowly etched the scrolling floral design on the tumbler as I quietly drank my very first glass of the smoky chicory coffee.

I'm not sure if it was the percolating sound of the coffeemaker puttering away or the smoky aroma that beckoned us out of our beds, but whatever it was, it brought us together in the mornings. Now, no matter how far I am from Grannie's kitchen table, I sit with my morning cup of coffee and the comfort of knowing my loved ones are taking part in the same daily ritual that connects us.

CAYENNE-CRUSTED WHOLE FRIED OKRA WITH CHIVE SAUCE

Serves 4

This recipe converted my husband. For his entire life, he swore off okra. (I'm not sure he ever tried it before claiming his hatred for the vegetable.) But one fateful July day, I fried a small batch of the season's first okra offerings for myself. I piled the okra onto a plate alongside a small mason jar filled with chive sauce. I turned my back for a moment to transfer my frying oil into a small container to cool, only to return to an empty plate! Michael stared at me for a moment and stated we must go back to the farmers' market to get more okra. I pretended to be upset that he ate my fried okra; secretly I was thrilled he was an okra convert.

When choosing okra to fry whole, look for small pods no longer than the length of your pinky finger. Small pods are best for frying whole and roasting; long pods the length of your index finger are better for skillet-frying (page 133).

1½ cups buttermilk

2 cups yellow cornmeal

½ teaspoon cayenne pepper

Kosher salt and freshly ground black pepper

1 pound fresh okra

Peanut oil, for frying

Chive Sauce (page 91)

Set up a dredging station in two shallow dishes. Place the buttermilk in one dish. Place the cornmeal and cayenne in the second dish. Season both with salt and black pepper and stir to combine.

Dip the okra into the buttermilk and dredge in the cornmeal, shaking off the excess. Set aside on a plate.

In a large cast iron or heavy-bottomed skillet, heat 2 inches of oil over medium heat to 350°F. Line a plate with paper towels.

Working in batches, fry the okra until golden, 2 to 3 minutes. Drain the fried okra on the paper towels and season lightly with salt. Serve with Chive Sauce and devour immediately.

CHIVE SAUCE

Makes about ¾ cup

This sauce will keep in the fridge for a few days. You may need to thin it out with a few drops of water, as it thickens up a bit when it's cold.

½ cup mayonnaise

1 garlic clove, finely chopped

2 tablespoons chopped chives

1 tablespoon plus 1 teaspoon red wine vinegar

Kosher salt and freshly ground black pepper

In a small bowl, whisk together the mayonnaise, garlic, chives, vinegar, and 1 tablespoon plus 1 teaspoon water. (Alternatively, shake everything together in a jar with lid.) Season with salt and pepper.

PIMENTO HUSHPUPPIES WITH SWEET WHIPPED BUTTER

Makes 12 hushpuppies

There is a ritual to eating piping hot hushpuppies. Split the hushpuppy in half with a butter knife, slather one half with sweet whipped butter, eat, and repeat until they are all gone.

1 cup medium-grind
  yellow cornmeal
1 tablespoon self-rising
  flour or all-purpose flour
½ teaspoon baking powder
¼ teaspoon baking soda
1 teaspoon kosher salt
2 tablespoons sugar
1 large egg, lightly beaten
½ cup cold sparkling water
2 tablespoons whole milk
1 tablespoon chopped
  pimentos, drained, or
  chives
Peanut oil, for frying
Sweet Whipped Butter
  (recipe follows)

In a medium bowl, whisk together the cornmeal, flour, baking powder, baking soda, salt, and sugar. In a smaller bowl, whisk together the egg, sparkling water, milk, and pimentos. Add the egg mixture to the cornmeal mixture and combine thoroughly. Cover and transfer to the fridge to rest for at least 30 minutes or up to 2 hours.

In a medium heavy-bottomed pot, heat 2 inches of the oil over medium heat to 360°F. Line a plate with paper towels. Working in batches of 4, drop rounded tablespoons of batter into the oil (I use a 1½-tablespoon scoop). Allow both sides to turn deeply golden brown, about two minutes total. Drain the fried hushpuppies on the paper towels.

Serve piping hot with the whipped butter.

SWEET WHIPPED BUTTER

Makes ⅔ cup

½ **cup heavy (whipping) cream**
Sea salt

In a stand mixer fitted with the whisk attachment, whisk the cream and a small pinch of sea salt on high speed until the cream churns into lovely whipped butter. Stash away in the fridge until you are ready to serve.

HUSHPUPPY HOARDER

During the summer, the hot, humid Louisiana air is heavy with mosquitoes, fireflies, and the scent of fried fish. Newspaper-shrouded picnic tables are piled high with platters of golden, crispy fish fillets and pale green peppery coleslaw; but peeking out from behind the Tabasco and rémoulade sauce rests my crowning joy of the fish fry: hushpuppies.

When I was young, I knew I was walking into a seafood restaurant because of the distinct aroma of damp wood and fish. There were moss-covered tanks filled with live seafood, and stuffed alligators to entertain my sisters and me while we waited for our table. I listened to everyone discuss what they were going to order. Whenever I was asked what I wanted, I simply stated, "Nothing." But I had a plan. Most people go to seafood restaurants because of the seafood, naturally, but I adore going to seafood restaurants for the bottomless basket of hushpuppies.

When we sat down at our table, I immediately grabbed the boat-shaped, woven basket filled with brown paper and tiny, round golden hushpuppies and placed them in front of me. Fishing out my trusty butter knife from its paper restrainer, I cut the piping hot, golden nugget of fried cornbread in half, allowing the sweet steam to escape. I grabbed a small packet of butter from the center of the table, where it sat alongside the hot sauce, salt, and pepper (as if butter was like any other condiment), and with very precise motions, I slathered half the packet on half of the hushpuppy and the rest on the other half . . . and popped both halves into my mouth.

Once I finished one little basket of several hushpuppies, I replaced the empty basket where I found it and stealthily made my way over to the other side of the table, which had a full basket of untouched hushpuppies. Dodging the juices of cracking crab legs, I reached for more hushpuppies, which were in sheer peril of being contaminated by seafood spatter. I repeated this throughout the entire meal without any adults even noticing. No one would guess that I ate my weight in hushpuppies. Quiet and content, I sat at the end of the table with a pile of spent butter packets in front of me and a whisper of a smile running across my face. *Hushpuppies.*

SPICY ROSEMARY PECANS

Makes 4 cups

This is a great recipe to make ahead of time because the pecans become more flavorful as they sit in the fridge.

---

4 cups pecan halves
3 tablespoons extra-virgin olive oil
1 tablespoon finely chopped rosemary
Pinch of cayenne pepper
Kosher salt and freshly ground black pepper

Preheat the oven to 350°F.

Place the pecan halves on a rimmed baking sheet. Toast until the pecans begin to give off a nutty aroma, about 8 minutes.

Meanwhile, in a medium bowl, whisk together the olive oil, rosemary, cayenne, and salt and black pepper to taste.

Toss the hot pecans into the bowl as soon as they come out of the oven. Stir until the pecans are fully coated. At this point, you can devour the pecans or store them in an airtight bag in the refrigerator for later use. They keep for a few weeks in the fridge. Bring the pecans to room temperature before serving.

VARIATION

Brown Butter and Sage Pecans: Brown butter and sage add a wonderful meatiness to pecans. Place a small ovenproof skillet over medium-low heat. Place 3 tablespoons unsalted butter in the skillet, remove from the heat, and swirl it around until it melts. Return the skillet to the heat. After a few minutes, the butter will turn golden and a lovely nutty aroma will fill your kitchen. Take the skillet off the heat and add 3 sage leaves. Allow the leaves to gently fry for 30 seconds. Transfer the warm butter to a medium mixing bowl, discard the sage leaves, and whisk in salt and pepper to taste. Toss the warm pecans in the butter and serve immediately, or stash in the fridge for a few weeks and rewarm before serving.

WHITE CHEDDAR AND ROSEMARY CHEESE WAFERS

Makes about 28 cheese wafers

I'm giving you fair warning: These cheese wafers are quite addictive. They taste just like traditional Southern cheese straws, but the method is simplified—no need for a fancy cookie press. Just slice, bake, and serve.

10 ounces sharp white cheddar cheese, finely shredded, at room temperature

1½ cups all-purpose flour

8 tablespoons (1 stick) unsalted butter, at room temperature

1 teaspoon kosher salt

1 teaspoon freshly ground black pepper

1 teaspoon finely chopped rosemary

1 teaspoon red pepper flakes

2 tablespoons heavy (whipping) cream

In a food processor, combine the cheese, flour, butter, salt, black pepper, rosemary, and red pepper flakes and pulse until the mixture resembles coarse sand. Add the cream and continue pulsing until the dough comes together to form a ball. Shape the dough into a log, roughly 2 inches in diameter, and wrap in plastic wrap or parchment paper. Chill for at least 3 hours and up to 12 hours.

Preheat the oven to 350°F. Line two large baking sheets with parchment paper.

Cut the dough into ¼-inch-thick rounds. Place the rounds on the prepared baking sheets and bake until golden brown around the edges, 16 to 18 minutes. (If you have a tiny oven or only 1 large baking sheet, simply bake these wafers in 2 batches.)

These wafers are irresistible while they are still warm, but they are delicious when cooled as well. They can be made up to 2 weeks in advance. Store cooled wafers in an airtight container at room temperature.

VARIATION

Cajun-Spiced Cheese Wafers: Substitute ½ teaspoon fresh thyme leaves for the finely chopped rosemary, and 1 teaspoon cayenne pepper plus ½ teaspoon smoked sweet paprika for the red pepper flakes.

ROSEMARY AND SEA SALT POTATO CHIPS

Serves 4

Rinsing the potatoes, soaking them in vinegar, and frying them at a lower temperature result in a perfectly crisp chip! These are lovely served with the Chive Sauce (page 91).

Leaves from 2 sprigs
   rosemary, finely chopped
   (about 1 heaping
   tablespoon)
1 tablespoon sea salt
1½ pounds russet (baking)
   potatoes, scrubbed
½ cup distilled white
   vinegar
Peanut oil, for frying

In a small bowl, mix the rosemary and sea salt. Rub the mixture together with your fingertips, infusing the rosemary oils into the sea salt. Set aside.

Slice the potatoes ⅛ inch thick using a mandoline with the safety guard. If you don't have a mandoline, carefully slice the potatoes using a very sharp knife.

Toss the potato slices into a salad spinner. Cover them with cold water. Swish the potatoes around with your fingertips and drain the potatoes. Rinse the potatoes a few times until the water is clear and no longer cloudy. Fill the salad spinner with fresh, cold water and add the vinegar. Let the potatoes sit in the vinegar water for 30 minutes. Drain and spin the potatoes dry in the salad spinner.

Meanwhile, in a large heavy-bottomed pot, heat 2 to 3 inches of peanut oil over medium heat to 325°F. Line a plate with paper towels.

Carefully place a handful of potato slices into the oil, making sure not to crowd the pot. Fry until lightly golden and crisp, 3 to 5 minutes, then drain on the paper towels. Immediately sprinkle lightly with the rosemary–sea salt mixture. Continue frying the rest of the potato slices. These chips are best eaten immediately, but they can also be stored in an airtight bag on the counter for a day.

PIMENTO CHEESE AND THYME GOUGÈRES

Makes about 24 gougères

These pimento-studded cheese puffs are a lovely appetizer to serve with wine or cocktails. Keep in mind the gougère dough can be made 4 hours ahead. Cover and chill until ready to use.

8 tablespoons (1 stick) unsalted butter, cut into cubes

1 teaspoon kosher salt

½ cup whole milk

1 cup all-purpose flour

1 jar (4 ounces) diced pimentos, drained

4 large eggs, plus 1 egg yolk for brushing

1½ cups finely shredded sharp cheddar cheese

½ teaspoon fresh thyme leaves

½ teaspoon freshly ground black pepper

¼ teaspoon cayenne pepper

Preheat the oven to 400°F. Line a baking sheet with parchment paper.

In a medium saucepan, combine the butter, salt, milk, and 1 cup water. Bring to a boil over medium heat, stirring constantly for 1 minute to keep it from boiling over. Add the flour and beat vigorously with a wooden spoon for another minute until the mixture is smooth and pulls away from the sides of the pan, forming a ball.

Reduce the heat to low, stirring constantly for 2 minutes. At this point, the dough will begin to dry out. Remove from the heat and let rest for 5 minutes.

Meanwhile, finely chop the pimentos and place on a small plate lined with a paper towel.

One at a time, add the 4 whole eggs to the slightly cooled dough, stirring well between each addition. At this point, the dough will look sloppy and you will feel as if you have completely ruined it, but trust me. Just keep stirring until the dough becomes smooth. Add the pimentos, cheese, thyme, black pepper, and cayenne. Keep stirring until all the ingredients are incorporated.

On the lined baking sheet, create 1-inch mounds of dough, 2 inches apart, either by piping the dough using a piping bag, or using a small cookie dough scoop or a tablespoon. Whisk the egg yolk and 1 teaspoon of water and brush the egg wash onto the gougères.

Bake until puffed and golden, 25 to 30 minutes. Serve warm.

BOUDIN BALLS WITH RAVIGOTE SAUCE

Makes 16 to 18 boudin balls

This is my favorite way to enjoy boudin. The hot, crisp crust breaks, revealing tender, steaming spiced pork and rice. These are best eaten with your fingers, but you can use a fork if you must. Dip the boudin balls in the ravigote sauce or simply drag a piping hot boudin ball across a mound of Creole mustard.

½ pound boneless pork chops, cut into 1-inch cubes

¼ medium red onion, finely chopped

1 serrano pepper, seeded and finely chopped

3 green onions (scallions), white and pale green parts only, finely sliced

2 garlic cloves, finely chopped

½ teaspoon cayenne pepper

¼ teaspoon chili powder

¼ teaspoon smoked sweet paprika

Kosher salt and freshly ground black pepper

In a quart-size plastic bag, combine the pork, onion, serrano pepper, green onions, garlic, cayenne, chili powder, smoked paprika, 1½ teaspoons kosher salt, ½ teaspoon black pepper, and chipotle pepper sauce. Rub all the ingredients together. Marinate in the fridge for at least 1 hour or up to 12 hours.

Transfer the pork and vegetables to a medium saucepan and add water to cover by 2 inches. Bring to a boil over medium-high heat, reduce the heat to low, and simmer, partially covered, for 2 hours. Remove from the heat and pour into a sieve set over a bowl. Measure out ¾ cup plus 2 tablespoons of the poaching liquid and set aside. Transfer the pork to a food processor and pulse a few times. The boudin mixture should resemble a loose sausage mixture.

Transfer the boudin mixture to a stand mixer fitted with the flat beater attachment. Add the rice, parsley, and reserved poaching liquid and mix on a low speed for 5 minutes. The boudin will be a little loose, but this ensures the rice will not dry out as the boudin cooks later. Cover and

A few dashes of Tabasco
   chipotle pepper sauce
1¾ cups Steamed Rice
   (page 28), at room
   temperature
1 tablespoon finely
   chopped parsley leaves
½ cup all-purpose flour
2 large eggs
¾ cup dried breadcrumbs
Peanut oil, for frying
Ravigote Sauce (page 107)
   or Creole mustard

refrigerate the boudin mixture until completely cool, or up to 12 hours if you want to make the boudin ahead of time.

Set up a dredging station in 3 shallow dishes. Scoop the flour into one dish, crack and lightly beat the eggs in a second, and pour the breadcrumbs into the third dish. Season each lightly with salt and pepper. Create boudin balls by scooping the mixture into 1½-tablespoon balls. (I use a 1½-tablespoon cookie dough scoop.) Gently roll the boudin balls between your palms. Roll each ball in flour, then toss in the egg. Shake off any excess egg and roll in the breadcrumbs. Place the boudin balls on a platter.

In a medium heavy-bottomed pot, heat 2 inches of peanut oil over medium heat to 350° to 360°F. Line a plate with paper towels.

Working in a few batches, fry the boudin balls until golden brown, 3 to 5 minutes. Drain on the paper towels. Serve immediately with ravigote sauce or Creole mustard.

VARIATION

Boudin Links: You can use the Boudin Ball mixture to make boudin links (it makes approximately 1½ pounds; nine links). Once stuffed into casings, poach the links in gently simmering water for 10 minutes. Serve the poached boudin with Creole mustard and Ravigote Sauce (recipe follows).

RAVIGOTE SAUCE

Makes about ½ cup

I was first introduced to ravigote sauce in New Orleans. It is usually served with crabmeat, but I find that the acidity and spice in this sauce complements the fried boudin balls beautifully.

¼ cup mayonnaise
Juice of ½ lemon
½ teaspoon Creole or
  whole-grain mustard
½ teaspoon white wine
  vinegar
1 teaspoon prepared
  horseradish
Pinch of cayenne pepper
Pinch of smoked sweet
  paprika
Kosher salt and freshly
  ground black pepper

In a small bowl, whisk together the mayonnaise, lemon juice, mustard, vinegar, horseradish, cayenne, and paprika. Season with salt and black pepper and adjust the other seasonings to your taste. Cover and refrigerate until you are ready to serve.

SIDES

LADY PEA SALAD

Serves 4

This recipe also works wonderfully with fresh or frozen black-eyed peas, if you can't find lady peas.

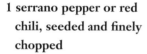

1 serrano pepper or red chili, seeded and finely chopped

1 garlic clove, finely chopped

1 tablespoon finely chopped mint leaves

1 tablespoon finely chopped basil leaves, plus a few whole leaves for garnish

¼ cup olive oil

2 tablespoons apple cider vinegar

2 tablespoons fresh lemon juice

Kosher salt and freshly ground black pepper

2 cups fresh or frozen lady peas

Extra-virgin olive oil, to finish

In a medium bowl, whisk together the serrano pepper, garlic, mint, basil, olive oil, vinegar, and lemon juice. Season with salt and pepper. Cover the dressing and refrigerate while you prepare the lady peas.

In a medium saucepan, combine the lady peas and 3 cups cold water. Bring to a boil over medium heat, then reduce to a simmer, partially cover, and cook until the beans are tender, about 30 minutes. Stir occasionally, skimming any natural foam that rises to the top.

Drain the lady peas, transfer to the bowl with the vinaigrette, and toss. Scatter a few more basil leaves on top and finish with a drizzle of extra-virgin olive oil. This salad can be prepared ahead of time, simply cover and refrigerate for up to two days. Bring to room temperature before serving.

EVERYDAY CUCUMBER SALAD

Serves 4

This simple cucumber salad graced our table daily alongside sliced tomatoes and canta-loupe. We always peel our cucumbers, then take a salad fork and score the length of the flesh with the tines. This scoring creates a lovely pattern around the edges of the cucum-ber slices and tiny crevices for the vinegar and seasonings to fill.

2 large cucumbers, peeled and scored (see above)
White wine vinegar
Kosher salt and freshly ground black pepper

Cut the scored cucumbers into ⅛-inch-thick slices. Arrange the cucumbers on a plate and lightly drizzle with vinegar. Season with salt and pepper.

THE ENCHANTED CUCUMBER PATCH

During the long, hot summer months, our backyards were treasure troves of edible gems. A portion of each neighbor's yard was a garden of sorts, revealing characteristics of its caretaker. Some gardens overflowed with herbs and spring onions in simple clay pots, others with emerald green bell pepper plants in perfectly straight rows. The more adventurous gardeners had a few chickens strutting about their yards, feasting away on herbs and fallen vegetables. Then, there were those who created raised vegetable beds out of old barbecue pits and tractor tires.

I remember tending to our backyard garden with my mom when I was a little girl. One night, I sat in the dirt next to the cucumber plants as we began snipping a few green onions for our dinner. I couldn't help but stare at the perfectly ripe cucumbers suspended in midair, reminding me of sausages hanging in a meat market. I looked under one of the jade leaves and spotted a small cucumber with a bright yellow flower attached at one end. A crack of thunder in the distance broke my focus. Tomato plants swayed in the breeze and drops of cool summer rain began hitting our cheeks. "Be sure to peek at this one in the morning," Mom said with a knowing smile. Before it began pouring, we rushed inside with fists and arms full of green onions and cucumbers. I thought no more of the tiny cucumber and continued helping to prepare for dinner.

The next morning, I walked outside to gather a few tomatoes and herbs for breakfast. I remembered what my mom told me about the baby cucumber, so I began folding the leaves back, and, lo and behold, the teeny cucumber grew half the length of my forearm overnight. I couldn't believe it! From that moment on, I thought of cucumbers as being enchanted. They appear mystically in our garden patch after a midsummer storm and disappear just as magically at our table.

ROASTED STUFFED PEPPERS WITH TOMATOES AND BASIL

Serves 4

Creole tomatoes are simply tomatoes grown in Louisiana soil, picked ripe from the vine and sold the same day. Creole tomatoes are deformed, imperfect, and delicious. Since I can't find Creole tomatoes in Nashville, I pay homage to the tradition of the Creole tomato by finding the best local tomatoes, peppers, and chilies for this lovely summer dish. Before you slice the chilies, taste a tiny bit to see how much of the chili you want to add. If your skin is sensitive to chilies, put on gloves before handling.

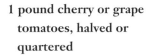

1 pound cherry or grape tomatoes, halved or quartered

1 small garlic clove, thinly sliced

1 hot red chili or serrano pepper, seeded and thinly sliced

1 mild chili, such as banana pepper, seeded and thinly sliced

1 tablespoon red wine vinegar

2 tablespoons olive oil, plus more for serving

Sea salt

Small handful of basil leaves

4 medium bell peppers, halved lengthwise through the stem and seeded

Preheat the oven to 425°F.

In a medium bowl, combine the tomatoes, garlic, chilies, vinegar, olive oil, and salt. Set aside a few small basil leaves for garnish and add the remainder to the bowl. Use your fingers to scrunch the ingredients together. Taste and adjust the vinegar, oil, and salt. Set aside.

Place the bell peppers cut side up in a roasting pan. Season the inside of each cavity with salt.

Use your hands to fill the bell peppers with the filling, coaxing the tomatoes and chilies into the corners of the bell peppers. Make sure to pour any of the lovely juice that pools at the bottom of the bowl over the top of the bell peppers.

Cover the pan with foil and bake for 30 minutes. Remove the foil and bake until the peppers are soft, about another 30 minutes. Sprinkle the reserved basil leaves on top of the roasted peppers and serve.

OREGANO AND GARLIC BUTTER BEANS

Serves 4

My mother would recite the same thoughts out loud every time we had company coming for dinner: "Oh, I forgot to ask if they like butter beans. No worries, Amber will eat any leftovers." And she was right. I can eat my weight in butter beans. I love my butter beans spicy, sharp, and garlicky.

1 pound fresh or frozen butter beans (lima beans)

½ head garlic, cloves separated and peeled

2 tablespoons olive oil

Generous pinch of red pepper flakes

Leaves from 1 sprig oregano (or ½ teaspoon dried oregano)

Red wine vinegar

Kosher salt and freshly ground black pepper

In a medium saucepan, combine the butter beans, garlic, oil, red pepper flakes, and 2 cups cold water. Bring to a boil over medium heat, reduce the heat to a simmer, partially cover, and cook over low heat until the beans are tender, about 15 minutes. Once the beans are tender, take the pot off the heat. Cover and allow the beans to sit in the poaching liquid for 10 minutes.

Squish the garlic along with a few beans against the side of pot. (The squished beans will make the dish creamy without the addition of cream or butter.) Add the oregano and season to taste with vinegar, salt, and black pepper. Keep the beans covered in the warm cooking liquid until ready to serve.

AUGUST MORNINGS

Early August mornings began with a short stroll to my grandma's small garden patch. I remember walking barefoot in the grass and the feeling of the cool blades, still wet with morning dew. A sheltering fig tree filled the patch with a pleasant aroma of honey. Blackberries hid under their leaves like treasures waiting to be discovered, and sunny yellow flowers beamed at me with ruby eyes from the towering okra stalks. Delicate jade fingers slowly swayed back and forth in the breeze, quietly summoning me like a queen giving consent to approach her throne. Peppery, grassy scents filled the air as I clicked an okra pod the size of my pinky off its resting place, tossed it into a bucket, and quickly filled the container to the brim with these emerald jewels. I followed the trail back to the house with a pail full of okra nestled in my arms and the promise of a lovely summer's day.

SPICY ROASTED OKRA

Serves 4

Cutting the okra in half lengthwise and roasting it eradicates the "slimy" texture that most people associate with okra. Also, look for okra no longer than the length of your pinky finger. These smaller ones are delicate, which are perfect for this recipe.

---

1 pound okra
½ teaspoon kosher salt
¼ teaspoon freshly ground black pepper
½ teaspoon red pepper flakes
¼ cup olive oil

Preheat the oven to 400°F.

Trim the top and bottom tips off the okra pods and halve the okra lengthwise.

In a medium bowl, toss together the okra, salt, black pepper, red pepper flakes, and olive oil until well combined. On a rimmed baking sheet or in a cast iron skillet, spread the okra in a single layer and roast in the oven until golden brown and crispy, 15 to 20 minutes. (If you use a cast iron skillet, the okra will get crispy a lot faster, so check it after 10 minutes.) Serve immediately.

MAQUE CHOUX

Serves 4 to 6

Maque choux (pronounced mock-shoe) is a lovely Cajun side dish, which is inspired by a Native American recipe. Think of it as a Cajun version of succotash!

---

2 slices thick-cut bacon

1 small red onion, finely chopped

1 serrano pepper, seeded and finely chopped

½ teaspoon smoked sweet paprika

Pinch of red pepper flakes

Kosher salt and freshly ground black pepper

2 medium tomatoes, peeled (see Tips), seeded, and finely diced

3 garlic cloves, finely chopped

1½ cups hot water

6 ears corn, husked and kernels removed (see Tips)

Small handful of basil leaves

In a large cast iron or heavy-bottomed skillet, cook the bacon over medium-high heat until crispy and golden brown. Remove the bacon from the skillet and drain on a paper towel.

To the bacon drippings, add the onion, serrano pepper, smoked paprika, and red pepper flakes. Season lightly with salt and black pepper. Sauté over medium-high heat for 5 minutes. Add the tomatoes, garlic, and hot water. Season lightly with salt. Bring to boil, then reduce to a simmer and cook for 10 minutes.

Add the corn and simmer until the corn is tender, another 15 minutes. Take off the heat. Crumble in the bacon and stir in the basil leaves. Adjust the seasoning. Serve immediately.

Tips: To remove the kernels, lay the corn flat on a cutting board. Hold the cob with one hand, and with the other carefully cut a few rows of kernels down the side of the cob, creating a flat surface so the cob doesn't roll around on the cutting board. Keep rotating the corn, cutting the kernels off the side of the cob. Once all the kernels have been cut off, stand the cob upright and use the back of the knife to scrape the cob in a downward motion, making sure you collect all the milky liquid that comes out of the cob.

To quickly peel the tomatoes, simply score the bottoms with an "x" and place them in a medium bowl. Cover the tomatoes with boiling water. Allow them to sit in the water for about 5 minutes, or until the skin splits and easily peels from the flesh of the tomato.

GLORIOUS ROASTED POTATOES WITH ROSEMARY AND PARMESAN

Serves 4

These beauties are quite addictive, and they will disappear in a matter of minutes. Breaking through these perfectly roasted potatoes—listening to the exaggerated crunch, inhaling the meaty aromatics, and allowing the creamy, fluffy insides of the potato to fall on your tongue like warm, buttery clouds—makes every second spent cooking them worthwhile.

2½ pounds Yukon Gold potatoes, peeled and quartered
Kosher salt
1 tablespoon unsalted butter
2 tablespoons olive oil
6 garlic cloves, unpeeled
2 rosemary sprigs
Freshly grated Parmesan cheese, for serving

Preheat the oven to 425°F.

Place the potatoes in a large pot and add cold water to cover by about 1 inch. Cover the pot and place over high heat. As soon as the water begins to boil, lightly season with salt. Boil the potatoes until fork-tender, about 5 minutes.

Meanwhile, place a large cast iron or ovenproof skillet in the preheated oven.

Drain the potatoes in a colander and allow them to steam for 3 minutes. Shake the colander until the potatoes start to look fuzzy around the edges. (This step helps create a crunchy roasted potato.)

Remove the preheated skillet from the oven and add the butter and olive oil. Rock the skillet back and forth, covering the entire surface of the skillet. Once the butter melts, toss the drained potatoes in the hot skillet, lightly season with salt, and place in the oven for 30 minutes; toss in the garlic and rosemary. Return to the oven and roast until the edges are crispy and golden brown, about 30 minutes longer.

Transfer the potatoes to a warm serving dish, shower the roasted potatoes with the grated Parmesan, and serve hot.

REAPING WHAT YOU SOW

Right down the street from where I lived was my tiny elementary school, sweetly nestled next to a convenience store and a beloved grocery store. Tucked in between the worn hurricane fence and the textured brick facade of the taupe-colored school was a modest plot of dirt where Mrs. Benoit's second-grade class conducted *very* important physical science experiments.

The entire group marched outside into the garden. We fashioned furrows with our hands, gently creating holes with our index fingers, and dropped tiny seeds into the hollows. We covered them with the dark soil, gave them a drink, and hoped they slept tight under the dirt and didn't let the bedbugs bite.

Over the course of a few weeks during recess, I took a quick peek at the petite garden. My heart filled with delight as I began seeing little sprigs of green hairs and emerald leaves pushing through the soil and stretching out in the sunlight like small children awakening after midafternoon naps.

Then, on one bright and sunny day, Mrs. Benoit told us to retreat to the adored garden we had been tending. She handed out little gardening gloves and assigned each student a row of veggies to harvest. I was assigned to a short row of mysterious emerald leaves, while the rest began plucking beautiful vibrant green cucumbers and zucchini off their vines. Immediately, I became chartreuse with envy but quickly shrugged it off and stayed on task.

Rising to the challenge, I lowered my gaze and confronted the bright green plant and gave it a good yank. Suddenly with a *zip* I flew onto my back, holding a clump of mud. I shook myself off, trying to clean the dirt from my clothes without attracting too much attention to myself. Then I stared at my fist and gasped, running over to Mrs. Benoit screaming, "I think I just harvested turtle eggs!" She laughed and said, "Honey, those are potatoes." My eyes became as big as golf balls in disbelief. I never looked at a gloriously humble potato the same way ever again.

SKILLET-FRIED OKRA

Serves 4

Grandpa, my dad's father, is the okra king in our family. He uses my great-grandmother's perfectly slick cast iron skillet to pan-fry rounds of just-picked okra from my grandparents' backyard. He has a heavy hand when adding the red pepper flakes and cooks the okra until it is just about to break down but is still a beautiful shade of emerald green. This recipe began years ago as smothered okra, but as the years went by he began cooking the okra at a higher temperature for less time, and it magically transformed into pan-fried okra. This is my version of my grandpa's pan-fried okra or, as we still call it, "smothered okra." This is a lovely side dish to serve alongside, or in, gumbo.

¼ cup olive oil

Generous pinch of freshly ground black pepper

Generous pinch of red pepper flakes

1 pound okra, cut crosswise on the diagonal into ½-inch rounds

2 garlic cloves, finely chopped

Kosher salt

In a large skillet, heat the olive oil over medium heat. Once the oil is hot, sprinkle in the black pepper and red pepper flakes. Let the seasonings infuse in the oil for 30 seconds. Toss in the okra. Cook the okra until golden brown around the edges, stirring every minute or so, 10 to 15 minutes. Take the skillet off the heat, add the garlic, season with salt, and toss. Serve immediately.

COMFORTING SCALLOPED POTATOES

Serves 4

This is an indulgent dish I serve alongside roasted meats on cold winter nights. I also serve it for dinner during warmer months with a green salad.

---

4 tablespoons unsalted butter, melted, plus more for greasing

Kosher salt

2 pounds Yukon Gold potatoes, peeled and cut into ¼-inch-thick slices

1 cup heavy (whipping) cream

1 cup whole milk

1 medium garlic clove, finely chopped

1 cup freshly grated Parmesan cheese

Freshly ground black pepper

Preheat the oven to 375°F. Generously grease a 12-inch baking dish or skillet with butter.

In a large pot of boiling salted water, cook the potatoes, covered, for 5 minutes. Drain in a colander and allow the potatoes to steam for 1 minute.

Return the potatoes to the pot and add the cream, milk, garlic, melted butter, and ½ cup of the Parmesan. Season with salt and pepper. Toss the ingredients together until the potatoes are well coated.

Layer the potatoes in the buttered baking dish. Pour any remaining liquid on top of the potatoes. Scatter the top with the remaining ½ cup Parmesan. Cover the baking dish with foil and bake for 40 minutes. Remove the foil and bake until golden brown, another 15 to 20 minutes.

PRACTICALLY PERFECT POPOVERS

Makes 6 large popovers

I've tried many popover recipes. Some recipes say to rest the batter for 30 minutes, others overnight in the fridge, and some blend up the cold ingredients and pour the batter straight in the popover pan. But I found the results to be hit-or-miss. Some popovers rose to towering heights, then immediately deflated when they came out of the oven. Others had wonderful flavor, but they were a bit heavy and custardy in the middle. In this recipe, the popovers don't need time to rest, but the batter must be warm. They rise beautifully and keep their shape after they come out of the oven and are delightfully hollow in the middle. These popovers (pictured on page 108) are practically perfect every time.

1½ cups whole milk

2 large eggs, at room temperature

1½ teaspoons kosher salt

1½ cups all-purpose flour

2 tablespoons unsalted butter, melted

Line a rimmed baking sheet with foil. Place a popover pan on the baking sheet and transfer to the oven. Preheat the oven to 425°F.

Meanwhile, in a medium saucepan, heat the milk over low heat. Take off the heat just before the milk comes to a simmer. Whisk the eggs into the warm milk for about 1 minute. Add the salt and flour and whisk until the batter is smooth. The batter will be thinner than pancake batter but thicker than crêpe batter. Transfer the batter to a 4-cup measuring cup. (This will make it easier to pour the batter into the popover pan.)

Once the oven preheats, take the popover pan out of the oven and brush the bottom and sides of the popover cups with the melted butter. (Reserve any extra butter for brushing the popovers later.) Return the pan to the oven for 3 minutes.

Pour the warm batter into the cups, filling them one-half to three-quarters full. (You may end up with a little bit of batter left over, but it's important not to overfill the popover cups as it will result in a custardy center, not a hollow one.)

Bake until deeply golden brown, 30 to 35 minutes. (Do not open the oven! If you must check on them, use the oven light.)

Invert the popovers onto the baking sheet. Brush the popovers with the reserved melted butter and serve immediately. Any leftover popovers can be stored at room temperature in an airtight container for one to two days.

VARIATIONS

Pimento Cheese Popovers: To the prepared popover batter, fold in ½ cup grated cheddar cheese and ¼ cup drained and diced jarred pimento peppers until just combined. Transfer to the popover pan and bake as directed.

Sugar and Spice Popovers: Popovers are lovely as a savory side, but I also serve a sweetened version for breakfast or dessert. In a bowl, mix together about ¼ cup Superfine Vanilla Sugar (page 28) and 1 teaspoon ground cinnamon. After the baked popovers have been brushed with butter, roll them in the cinnamon sugar. Eat immediately!

BACON-STUDDED CORNBREAD

Serves 6 to 8

Some Southerners believe it's sacrilegious to add sugar to cornbread batter, but I grew up eating cornbread with a spoonful of sugar. I love serving cornbread with greens and eggs for a light lunch, for dinner alongside hearty soups and stews, and with berries, cold milk, and sugar for dessert. If there are any leftover slices of cornbread, spilt them in half and toast both sides in a skillet and serve with Sweet Whipped Butter (page 93), preserves, and chicory coffee for breakfast.

2 slices thick-cut bacon, finely chopped

2 cups medium-grind yellow cornmeal

1½ teaspoons kosher salt

2½ teaspoons baking powder

1 tablespoon raw cane sugar

1¼ cups buttermilk

3 large eggs, lightly beaten

3 tablespoons unsalted butter, melted and cooled

1 tablespoon sunflower oil

Preheat the oven to 450°F. Place a 10-inch cast iron skillet in the oven to preheat.

In a small skillet, cook the chopped bacon over medium-low heat until the fat is rendered and the bacon bits are crispy. (Reserve 3 tablespoons of bacon fat. If you don't have enough fat, make up the difference with additional melted unsalted butter.) Drain the bacon bits on a small plate lined with a paper towel.

In a medium bowl, combine the cornmeal, salt, baking powder, and sugar. In a small bowl, combine the buttermilk, eggs, melted butter, and the reserved bacon fat. Add the buttermilk mixture to the cornmeal and stir to combine. Fold in the bacon bits.

Remove the preheated skillet from the oven. Add the sunflower oil, and swirl to coat the bottom and sides of the skillet. Pour in the thick batter. It should sizzle! Smooth the top of the batter.

Return the skillet to the oven and bake the cornbread until the top is golden brown and a toothpick inserted in the center comes out clean, 20 to 25 minutes. (I flip my cornbread once it comes out of the oven, but it's not necessary. This is purely to show off that golden crust.) Slice into wedges and serve straight from the skillet. Store any leftovers in an airtight container in the fridge.

VARIATION

Sweet Cornbread: Render the bacon fat but omit the bacon bits from the cornbread batter, and continue baking as directed. (Wrap up the drained bacon bits, stash them in the fridge, and toss them into an omelet or a salad.) To serve, place a warm wedge of cornbread upside down in the center of a shallow bowl, sprinkle with ½ teaspoon Superfine Vanilla Sugar (page 28), pour ⅓ cup cold milk around the cornbread, and top with ¼ cup blackberries. The combination of hot, crispy cornbread, cold sweet milk, and tart blackberries is simply divine.

MAINS

TOMATO AND BACON SANDWICH WITH CHIPOTLE MAYONNAISE

Serves 1

This recipe is a grown-up version of my childhood go-to sandwich. If done correctly, a tomato sandwich can be one of the greatest pleasures in life. Since this recipe is simple and requires few ingredients, quality is key, so try to buy the best bread, tomatoes, and bacon that you can.

---

2 slices thick-cut bacon
2 slices sourdough bread
Chipotle Mayonnaise (recipe follows)
2 slices tomato (½ to ¾ inch thick)

In a medium skillet, fry the bacon over medium-low heat until crispy. Drain the bacon on a plate lined with a paper towel. Place the skillet back on the heat and toast up both sides of the bread in the bacon renderings until golden brown.

Spread a layer of the chipotle mayonnaise over one side of each piece of toast. Lay the slices of bacon on top of the mayonnaise. Lightly press down on the bacon, helping it adhere to the mayonnaise. Lay the tomato slices on top of the bacon. Crown the sandwich with the remaining piece of mayonnaise-slathered toast. Press down on the sandwich and cut on the diagonal. This sandwich is best enjoyed standing over the kitchen sink.

CHIPOTLE MAYONNAISE

Makes ¼ cup

¼ cup mayonnaise
Several dashes of Tabasco chipotle pepper sauce

In a measuring cup, combine the mayonnaise and chipotle pepper sauce. Any leftover mayonnaise can be stored in the refrigerator for another use.

A WONDERFUL TOMATO SANDWICH

There are many forms of cruel and unusual punishment in this world, and one of them is having to eat a sandwich left in a plastic bag in a kindergarten classroom until noon. There I sit, in my favorite faded blue jean shorts and white T-shirt, staring at my soggy, sorry excuse for a sandwich. Steam from the amalgamation of white bread and humidity fills the inside of the plastic bag. One by one, the snaps from the seal of the bag give way under the force of my fingertips. The smells of hot yellow mustard and moist bread with just a hint of hammy-ness fill my nostrils. Reluctantly, I eat my not-so-wonderful sandwich, while sadly staring at the bags of potato chips and chocolate chip cookies littering the cafeteria table. Oh, how I long for Lunchables!

By the time I get home, I am ravenous. Running off the bus and onto the lawn, I throw my backpack into the yard and give a good tug on the screen door of our house. I am in the fridge by the time I hear the screen door shut. *BANG!* I meticulously lay out the cast of characters on the speckled Formica countertop: Wonder bread, mayonnaise, and thick slices of juicy, ruby tomatoes. The butter knife leaves little rake impressions as I spread the heavenly mayonnaise across the supple white bread. Two generous slices of succulent tomatoes crown the bread, slightly overlapping at the edges. Taking one bite of the creamy tomato sandwich magically erases the lunch-time horror from earlier in the day. Life is good.

MY CHICKEN SALAD

Serves 4

In Louisiana, I grew up with rémoulade, which is a creamy, piquant mayonnaise-based sauce traditionally tossed with seafood and served over a bed of lettuce. My chicken salad recipe is inspired by this classic French dish. It's bright, acidic, and gets a lovely kick from the Creole mustard. These flavors complement the roasted chicken and parsley beautifully. I often pile chicken salad onto toasted bread and serve it open-face with pickles. If you choose to serve your chicken salad on toasted bread, warm the reserved chicken drippings and fry both sides of your bread in this flavorful fat. It's decadent and delicious.

---

4 bone-in, skin-on chicken thighs (about 1½ pounds)

Kosher salt

2 tablespoons sunflower oil

½ cup Homemade Mayonnaise (page 149)

2 teaspoons fresh lemon juice

1 tablespoon chopped parsley

Freshly ground black pepper

Preheat the oven to 425°F.

Lightly season the chicken with salt. Coat a medium cast iron or other heavy-bottomed skillet with the oil and set over medium heat. Once the oil is hot, gently place the chicken thighs in the skillet, skin side down, and panfry until the skin is golden and crisp and the kitchen begins to fill with a nutty aroma, 8 to 10 minutes. (You know it's time to flip the thighs when the skin completely releases from the bottom of the skillet.)

Flip the thighs, transfer the skillet to the oven, and roast until the thighs are deeply golden brown and the temperature of the thighs reaches 165°F, 25 to 30 minutes. Transfer the thighs to a plate to cool. (Reserve the golden chicken drippings for toasting bread, if desired.)

Meanwhile, prepare the mayonnaise and store it in the fridge until ready to use.

Once the chicken thighs are cool enough to handle, shred the meat with your fingers (discard the skin and bones). You should end up with about 2 cups of chicken.

In a medium bowl, toss together the chicken, chilled mayonnaise, lemon juice, and parsley. Season with salt and pepper and serve.

Chicken Salad Sandwich: Slather a generous helping of chicken salad between two slices of squishy white bread and add lots of cold, crisp iceberg lettuce.

HOMEMADE MAYONNAISE

Makes about 1¼ cups

You can manually whisk mayonnaise if you don't have a stand mixer. You just need a balloon whisk and nonreactive bowl. Make sure to place a damp towel under your bowl to help keep it in place as you whisk.

1 tablespoon white wine
   vinegar
1 tablespoon fresh lemon
   juice
1 egg yolk
Pinch of kosher salt
Pinch of sugar
½ teaspoon Creole, Dijon,
   or whole-grain mustard
1 cup sunflower oil

In a small bowl, mix together the vinegar and lemon juice.

In a stand mixer fitted with the whisk attachment, combine the egg yolk, salt, sugar, mustard, and 1 tablespoon of the vinegar-lemon mixture. Whisk for a few seconds until the mixture is light and frothy.

With the mixer on a medium speed add the oil, drop by drop, until you have added half of the oil. (I always pour the oil out of a small measuring cup so I know when I've added exactly half of it.) This is a slow process but can't be rushed. If the oil is added too quickly, the mayonnaise will break and the oil will end up pooling, resulting in a sloppy mess!

Add the remaining 1 tablespoon vinegar-lemon mixture. Incorporate the rest of the oil in a slow, steady stream. Once all the oil has been added, whisk for another minute, or until the mayonnaise is thick and pale in color. Keep covered in the fridge for up to one week.

I DID IT MY WAY

I've met many chicken salads I like, but none that I love. There's always too much of this and that: pecans, raw onions, celery, apples, raisins, or grapes. Others are drowned in a white pool of mayonnaise with the occasional cube of chicken floating about. Some cooks almost puree the chicken, which, to me, looks a lot like cat food. Then, I realized I was discrediting and scrutinizing chicken salad after chicken salad without attempting to make it the way I dreamt to find it in restaurants. I felt like a hypocrite. So, to find balance and justice in the world, at least on the topic of chicken salad, I got to work.

When I began brainstorming about chicken salad, I imagined the chicken being the star of the dish. It shouldn't be hidden or an afterthought. Since this is a stripped-down version, and there are so few ingredients, I make my own mayonnaise. When you make your own mayonnaise, you notice the difference instantly in color, texture, and flavor. Think of mayonnaise as a dressing for the roasted chicken.

I won't be pushy. I won't tell you this is better than the recipe for your Great Aunt Ina's famous chicken salad, which is securely hidden in the family safe. This is simply my chicken salad. If a rainbow-hued chicken salad is equivalent to a woman decked out in her Easter best—Sunday hat, makeup, hairspray, and layered strands of pearls—this is equivalent to a woman at the end of an honest day's work after she washes her face, takes a long bath, and slips on her silk robe. Simple and elegant.

RED BEANS AND RICE SOUP

Serves 4

I love using Tabasco chipotle pepper sauce as the smoky element in this dish instead of ham hocks. Also, the night before I make this soup, I simply tumble the dried kidney beans into a bowl and cover them with cold water before turning off the lights in my kitchen for the night. They need twelve hours to soak.

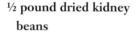

½ pound dried kidney beans

3 tablespoons olive oil

3 green onions (scallions), white and pale green parts only, finely sliced

1 medium red bell pepper, finely chopped

1 serrano pepper, seeded and finely chopped

1 medium red onion, finely chopped

4 garlic cloves, finely chopped

½ teaspoon dried oregano

½ teaspoon cayenne pepper

Kosher salt and freshly ground black pepper

A few dashes of Tabasco chipotle pepper sauce, plus more for serving

1 cup Steamed Rice (page 28), for serving

Extra-virgin olive oil, for finishing

Parsley leaves, for serving

Place the beans in a medium bowl and add cold water to cover by a few inches. Let the beans soak for twelve hours. Drain the beans, rinse, then drain again. Set the beans aside.

Bring a kettle filled with water to a boil so it's on hand. You will need it in a few minutes!

In a soup pot, heat the olive oil over medium heat. Once hot, add the green onions, bell pepper, serrano pepper, red onion, garlic, oregano, and cayenne. Lightly season with salt and black pepper. Cook the vegetables until tender, about 5 minutes. Toss in the kidney beans and chipotle pepper sauce. Add boiling water to cover by 4 inches and season with salt. Cover and bring to a boil, then reduce to a simmer, partially cover, and simmer until the beans are tender and have a creamy texture, 2½ to 3 hours. Occasionally stir the pot, making sure nothing is sticking to the bottom and the beans are covered by 2 inches of liquid; add more hot water if needed.

Use a ladle to remove about 1½ cups of the beans and liquid. Transfer to a blender and puree. (Alternatively, just smash the beans with the back of the spoon against the pot.) Return the pureed beans and simmer, uncovered, for another 15 minutes. Take the pot off the heat and adjust the seasoning. Serve with about ¼ cup steamed rice per bowl, drizzle with extra-virgin olive oil, sprinkle with parsley, and serve with more chipotle pepper sauce, if you like.

SWEET CORN BISQUE

Serves 4

This is a lovely way to enjoy sweet corn as its peak. I love dipping the crispy bacon in the hot soup, which in my opinion, is the most wonderful accompaniment in the world.

4 ears corn, husked

4 slices thick-cut bacon

2 tablespoons unsalted butter

1 medium onion, sliced

1 garlic clove, sliced

Pinch of red pepper flakes

Kosher salt

4 cups boiling water

½ cup heavy (whipping) cream

1 heaping tablespoon cornstarch

Freshly ground black pepper

Preheat the broiler on high for 5 minutes.

Lay 2 ears of corn on a rimmed baking sheet and set under the broiler. Rotate until the kernels are lovely and charred. (Alternatively, you can grill the corn in a dry cast iron skillet over medium-high heat.) Let the roasted corn cool for a few minutes.

Cut the kernels off the roasted and fresh ears of corn (see Tips, page 126).

In a medium soup pot, cook the bacon over medium heat until crispy. Drain the bacon on a small plate lined with a paper towel and set aside for serving.

Add the butter, onion, garlic, red pepper flakes, and a pinch of salt to the pot. Cook over medium heat, stirring often, until the onion has softened and becomes translucent. Add the corn and stir for 2 minutes until every kernel is shiny.

Add the boiling water and cream and season with salt. Cover, with the lid slightly askew, and bring to a boil. Reduce to a simmer and cook until the corn is tender, about 5 minutes (the cooking times vary depending on the freshness of the corn).

In a small cup, whisk together the cornstarch and 2 tablespoons cold water. Stir the cornstarch slurry into the soup to thicken it. Simmer with the lid slightly askew for 5 minutes more.

Puree the soup until smooth using an immersion blender. Strain the soup through a fine-mesh sieve into a large bowl and return the soup to the pot. Adjust the salt and pepper to taste. Ladle the soup into serving bowls. Serve a slice of the reserved crispy bacon on the rim of each bowl.

CHILI CON CARNE WITH PICKLED RED ONIONS

Serves 6

Living in the South, I've had my share of chili. While it was never my favorite dish, my husband loves it. I couldn't deprive my husband of one of his favorite meals, so I challenged myself to make a chili we would both love. The bowls of chili I've had over the years were made with ground chuck, which is traditional for chili, but it made this dish quite heavy. Heavy meals never agree with me, and my stomach never agrees with them. So, as I began thinking about a chili I would crave, I knew I needed to use ground sirloin. I skim the fat that rises to the surface as it cooks so it doesn't end up in our stomachs, making us feel as if we've swallowed anvils. The flavor comes from vibrant, fruity peppers and fresh spices; layers of texture are provided by the silky sirloin, creamy beans, and tomatoes. Each bowl is crowned with a little sour cream and neon-pink pickled onions. My husband loves adding cubes of cheddar cheese to the bottom of his bowl and ladling the hot chili over the cubes, which creates delicious pockets of melting cheese. Fair warning: this chili is spicy. If you are sensitive to heat, use a jalapeño instead of a serrano pepper and skip the habanero (or just use half).

Olive oil

1 pound ground sirloin

Kosher salt and freshly ground black pepper

1 medium habanero pepper, seeded and finely chopped

1 medium serrano pepper or jalapeño, seeded and finely chopped

1 large red onion, finely chopped

Coat the bottom of a large heavy-bottomed pot with olive oil and set over medium-high heat. Toss in the ground sirloin. Season it lightly with salt and black pepper. As the beef browns, break it up with a wooden spoon. Once the moisture evaporates and the beef begins to caramelize, add both chili peppers, the onion, and garlic. Season lightly with salt. Cook until the onions are soft and translucent, 5 to 8 minutes.

Add the Worcestershire sauce, tomato paste, cornstarch, smoked paprika, red pepper flakes, and chili powder to the pot. Give the ingredients a good stir. Add the pinto beans, cannellini beans, and hot water.

3 garlic cloves, finely
chopped
1 tablespoon
Worcestershire sauce
2 tablespoons tomato
paste
1 heaping tablespoon
cornstarch
1 teaspoon smoked sweet
paprika
½ teaspoon red pepper
flakes
½ teaspoon chili powder
1 can (15 ounces) pinto
beans, drained and
rinsed
1 can (15 ounces)
cannellini beans,
drained and rinsed
5 cups hot water
2 cans (28 ounces each)
whole tomatoes, drained
White cheddar cheese,
grated or cut into
½-inch cubes, for
serving
Sour cream, for serving
Pickled Red Onions
(page 161), for serving

Hand-crush the tomatoes in a bowl and add to the chili. Season with salt and black pepper. Bring to a boil, then reduce to a simmer and cook for 3 hours with the lid askew, stirring occasionally and skimming the surface of any oil. Adjust the seasoning, if necessary.

To serve, place a large pinch of cheddar into the bottom of each bowl, ladle the chili over the cheddar, and top with sour cream and a few slices of Pickled Red Onions (see page 161).

PICKLED RED ONIONS

Makes about 1 cup

If there are any leftovers, you can toss these pink pickled onions into loads of salads: hearty green salads, grain salads, or rich egg, chicken, or potato salads.

½ medium red onion, thinly sliced
Juice of 1 lime
Small pinch of kosher salt

In a small bowl, toss together the onion, lime juice, and salt and rub the onions together with your fingertips. Allow the onions to sit at room temperature for at least 30 minutes. You can make these a few hours or days ahead; store them in the fridge for up to three days. (The onions will become delicate in texture and almost fluorescent pink in color the longer they sit.)

AT-HOME SHRIMP BOIL

Serves 4

This is a nod to the grand outdoor boils I remember as a child. It is a scaled-down at-home version of a seafood boil. No seafood boil would be complete without small condiment bowls filled with white vinegar and black pepper at each place setting. (This may seem odd, but vinegar helps balance out the natural saltiness in seafood.) If it's crawfish season, feel free to substitute crawfish for shrimp. You can put the spices in a muslin bag if you don't like the idea of whole spices swimming around your stockpot. Also, I find blending the oil and the cayenne helps the pepper immediately infuse with the rest of the ingredients. If you have one of those large stockpots with the pasta insert for easy draining, this is a great time to use it. If not, no worries, just drain the seafood in a large colander set in the sink.

½ cup sunflower oil

2 tablespoons cayenne
   pepper

¼ cup kosher salt

4 bay leaves

1 tablespoon mustard
   seeds

2 tablespoons coriander
   seeds

1 tablespoon allspice
   berries

1 tablespoon black
   peppercorns

1 head garlic, halved
   through the equator

Juice of 1 lemon

1 pound small Yukon
   Gold potatoes

4 ears corn, husked and
   halved crosswise

2 pounds head-on shrimp

In a bowl, blend the oil, cayenne, and ½ cup water with a whisk or an immersion blender. Pour into a large stockpot along with 1 gallon water and the salt, bay leaves, mustard seeds, coriander seeds, allspice berries, peppercorns, garlic, lemon juice, potatoes, and corn. Cover and bring to a rolling boil over high heat. (The water needs to boil as aggressively as you would boil water to cook pasta.)

Once the potatoes are fork-tender, 5 to 8 minutes, add the shrimp, cover, and bring back to a boil. After the water comes back to a boil, cook the shrimp for 3 minutes. Take the pot off the heat and allow everything to sit in the hot poaching liquid until the shrimp are cooked through, 5 to 10 minutes.

Drain and serve piping hot!

A GREAT BOIL

The humid air was thick with the scent of bay leaves, allspice, and cayenne pepper. A gumbo pot the size of a galvanized trash can bubbled away with fresh seafood, golden corn, and blushing red potatoes. The sun slowly set over the flat, evergreen terrain of the Louisiana landscape. Mighty magnolias perfumed the air with their sweet floral scent.

With sheer determination and little upper body strength, I awkwardly hauled two old picnic tables out from under the covered porch. I kicked over any four-inch-high crawfish holes that got in my way in order to arrange the tables nose-to-nose, as straight as possible under the massive oak tree in my grandparents' backyard. Mosquitoes began to buzz around my ear telling me the tables were cockeyed. I swatted them away without blinking an eye. I was sure the crawfish were planning their secret attack to get me back for knocking down their homes, but alas, it was necessary. Whenever it came time to prepare for dinner, everyone in my family had a task; on the night of a boil, setting the table was my chore of choice. It was the one night of the week when the men did the "cooking," as they gathered around the steaming pot of seafood, occasionally adjusting the flame on the propane tank and arguing about college football. The women sat at the kitchen table with mugs of chicory coffee, catching up on the latest gossip. *Ahem.* I mean news. I focused on setting the tables. I took this very seriously. My job was to create an atmosphere for conversations to flow, for memories to be made.

Making my way back inside the house to the living room, I peeked behind my grandfather's weathered and worn brown leather chair, which forever smells of Old Spice aftershave. Behind the chair, a two-foot pile of newspapers was nestled in a chipped and bowing magazine rack. I grabbed as many as I could carry and made my way outside, lined the tables with yesterday's news, and staggered eight bright green and purple beer platters on the table for the seafood to be served in. (One platter was placed in the center of the table and was designated for the shells.) Every place setting had a small bowl filled with white vinegar and black pepper. Plastic cups were filled to the brim with ice, and two 2-liter bottles of Coca-Cola were placed at the end of each table along with rolls of paper towels.

The sound of seafood draining from their bath was our dinner bell. Within moments, heads and shells were piled onto the designated platter, tails were dipped in the vinegar, and everyone began washing down the spicy seafood with Coke. (We used both palms to hold our cups to our lips since our fingers were covered in spices.) I remember sitting at the end of one table, watching my family members enjoy one another's company and reveling in stories, both old and new. The table was the setting for us to retell our stories of the day, the place to share our hearts; where memories and traditions were passed from generation to generation. It was a place where people came hungry and left being filled with food, laughter, and love.

Daylight melted into dusk and the fireflies danced the Cajun two-step under the mighty oak that sheltered us. Accordions wailed in the distance and were accompanied by chirping frogs nearby. The table was cleared; the leftover shells were divvied among family members and would be used to make the most delicious seafood stock the next day. The large pot was cleaned and put away until the next boil. As I crumpled up the spice-soaked newspaper, I realized the conversation would never truly end, the moment would never fade, as long as I shared these precious memories and filled my home with the ingredients, scents, and recipes I fell in love with.

TROUT WITH PECANS

Serves 4

This is a take on Trout Amandine, the classic French dish served in many New Orleans restaurants. Pecans grow in our backyards, so it feels natural to use pecans instead of the more traditional almonds.

4 trout fillets
  (4 to 6 ounces each)
Kosher salt and freshly
  ground black pepper
½ cup all-purpose flour,
  for dredging
8 tablespoons (1 stick)
  unsalted butter
½ cup thinly sliced pecans
Juice of 1 lemon, plus
  wedges for serving
2 tablespoons finely
  chopped parsley leaves

Season both sides of the fillets with salt and pepper. Place the flour in a shallow bowl. Dredge both sides of the fillets in the flour, shaking off the excess.

In a large cast iron or heavy-bottomed skillet, melt 4 tablespoons of the butter over medium-high heat. Just as the butter melts, add the fillets and cook on each side until golden brown, about 3 minutes per side. Transfer the fish to 4 warm serving plates.

Add the remaining 4 tablespoons butter to the skillet and reduce the heat to medium-low. Swirl the pan and cook just until the butter begins to brown. Add the sliced pecans and stir constantly until gently toasted, about 3 minutes. Take off the heat and add the lemon juice and parsley. Spoon the sauce over the fish and serve with lemon wedges.

FISHING LESSONS

Being raised on the bayous of Louisiana, I was introduced to fishing at the age of five. I woke up at first light, threw on my favorite faded blue jean shorts and white T-shirt, and piled into Paw-Paw's old truck, which smelled curiously of shoeshine and plastic bait. Our rods and reels bounced happily in the back of the truck, and the jingling of hooks in the tackle box was the only sound breaking the sweet silence as we drove down the long, dusty road.

We spent a good hour trying to find our fishing spot, which we called our "honey hole." I remember wearing a puffy, sun-bleached red life vest that smelled of fish. My grandfather pointed out huge cypress trees with their "knees" sticking out of the water and sunbathing alligators as we ventured closer to the fishing hole. The life vest squished my face, making me look like I had the cheeks of a chipmunk. My ponytail blew in the wind, tears streamed from the corners of my eyes, and a huge smile was plastered across my face.

Finally, we reached our fishing spot. My grandfather uncovered white Styrofoam cups filled with dirt and fresh worms. He carefully baited the hooks with the slimy, squiggling creatures. We cast our lines and sat . . . and sat. One of the first lessons in fishing is patience. Lots and lots of patience. Which explains why my paw-paw has always loved fishing. He is one of the most patient people I have ever met. Someone who throws his line in, time and time again, expecting nothing in return almost every single time. Through the art of fishing, he taught me the key to success: You must be willing to sit still, steadfast, refusing to give up.

I watched as his eyes scanned the surface of the filmy water. Sometimes, I imagined him having X-ray vision and the ability to probe the depths of the murky water just by staring at it. (His name is Ray, so you can imagine the concrete evidence I felt I had to support my theory.) I sat in silence, beheading the tiny silver shiners we had bought earlier that morning in case the fish didn't have an appetite for worms. I couldn't stand the thought of

putting the bait on the hook while they were still alive, so I quickly chopped the head off each shiner and began to weave their bodies onto a hook. I convinced myself that it was more humane this way. Just as I began to build a makeshift guillotine from the tin top of a soda can, the corks attached to our poles began to bob, weave, and duck under the muddy water. Using quick, short movements, my paw-paw tugged at the rod as he reveled in his fishy prize with laughter and a toothy grin.

Patiently, he taught me how to unhook the fish from the line and place it in a wire cage that was tied to the outside of the boat. I sat next to the cage of fish and watched them dart back and forth. I loved the way the sunlight reflected off their iridescent scales. Once we caught enough fish to fry for dinner, we sped back to the old truck to load up. The tops of my legs were slightly sunburned and my white Keds were a little worse for the wear, but I didn't mind. We were returning as victors.

When we arrived at my grandparents' house, my paw-paw took our prizes to the shed and scaled, gutted, and filleted the fish with an electric knife, which in any other household would be used for carving the Thanksgiving turkey. The freshly cut fillets were escorted to the kitchen where they were lightly breaded and deep-fried in a cast iron skillet until golden and crispy.

Fireflies, mosquitoes, and the aroma of fried fish filled the summer air as we sat at our beloved wooden picnic table, which was cloaked with a red-and-white checkered cloth. A pile of gilded fillets crowned the center of the table, along with a pile of vinegary coleslaw, spicy rémoulade sauce, and piping hot hushpuppies. We joined hands, bowed our heads, and in his strong yet kind voice, my paw-paw began thanking God for the food we were about to receive. I remember appreciating this meal more than most, not just because I helped catch the fish, but also because I learned an important lesson that day. Life can change in the blink of an eye and a flick of the wrist, if you are patient enough to wait for it and persistent enough to keep casting your line. Amen.

ELEGANT SUMMER TOMATO PASTA

Serves 4

I make this dish at least once a week during the summer. It makes the most out of the beautiful heirloom tomatoes at the market, and it is a quick, easy dish to whip up at a moment's notice.

½ cup olive oil

Generous pinch of red pepper flakes

2 garlic cloves, thinly sliced

Freshly ground black pepper

4 cups assorted small heirloom tomatoes, halved or quartered

Handful of torn basil leaves

Kosher salt

1 pound spaghetti or bucatini

Freshly grated Parmesan cheese, for serving

Extra-virgin olive oil, for serving

Fill a large pot with water and bring to a boil over high heat.

Meanwhile, in a large skillet, heat the olive oil over medium heat. Once the oil is hot, add the red pepper flakes, garlic, and a pinch of black pepper and let the oil infuse with the seasonings for 30 seconds. Toss in the tomatoes and basil. Season with salt. Reduce the heat to medium-low. As the sauce simmers, the tomatoes will release their juices. Let the sauce continue to simmer while you cook the pasta.

Once the water comes to a boil, season it with salt and toss in the pasta. Cook the pasta until al dente. Reserve about ½ cup of the starchy pasta water and drain the pasta in a colander.

Add the reserved pasta water and the pasta to the tomatoes and toss to combine. Allow the pasta to finish cooking in the sauce for a few minutes. Adjust the seasoning of the tomato sauce, if needed.

Divide the pasta among four warm pasta bowls (see Tip) and top with Parmesan. Drizzle with extra-virgin olive oil and serve.

Tip: As I bring the pasta water to a boil, I preheat my oven to the lowest possible temperature and set four ovenproof pasta bowls inside. Once the oven preheats, turn it off and let the bowls sit in the oven until you are ready to serve. Serving pasta in warm pasta bowls may seem like an odd tip from a home cook, but this simple ritual keeps the pasta and sauce warmer longer, and there's something comforting about curling up with a warm bowl of pasta on the couch.

CUCUMBER CARBONARA

Serves 4

Cooking with cucumbers may seem unusual, but the freshness of the cucumber pairs beautifully with smoky bacon and the richness of the carbonara sauce. I like to serve this, and any pasta dish, in warm pasta bowls (see Tip, page 174).

Kosher salt

1 pound spaghetti

2 medium cucumbers, peeled or unpeeled

4 slices thick-cut bacon, chopped

Leaves from 2 oregano sprigs

1 teaspoon red pepper flakes

4 egg yolks

½ cup heavy (whipping) cream

1 heaping handful of freshly grated Parmesan cheese, plus more to finish

Freshly ground black pepper

Extra-virgin olive oil, to finish

In a large pot of salted boiling water, cook the pasta until al dente. Reserve ½ cup of the starchy pasta water and drain the pasta in a colander; set aside.

Meanwhile, quarter the cucumber, lengthwise. Remove the seeds and cut each quarter crosswise on the diagonal into ¼-inch-thick slices.

In a large skillet, cook the bacon over medium heat until golden and crispy. Toss in the cucumbers, oregano, and red pepper flakes. Season lightly with salt. Sauté a few minutes, until the cucumber has softened slightly.

In a small bowl, whisk together the egg yolks, cream, Parmesan, and black pepper to taste. Season lightly with salt. (Keep in mind the pasta water, bacon, and cheese are salty.)

Take the skillet off the heat for a minute or so. Once the aggressive sizzling subsides, add the egg-cheese mixture and the cooked spaghetti. Toss, dribbling in small amounts of the pasta water, just to loosen the sauce. Serve immediately in warm bowls, with a little more Parmesan, a drizzle of extra-virgin olive oil, and a dusting of black pepper.

BACON AND COLLARD GREEN PAPPARDELLE

Serves 4

Collards turn bright green and retain a beautiful texture when cooked quickly at a high temperature. I am hard pressed to find a more comforting dish than these bitter collards slicked with spicy, lemony cream tangled in a mess of pappardelle and bacon. When cutting the collard greens, make sure to cut them the same width as the pappardelle.

1 pound pappardelle

4 slices thick-cut bacon, chopped

½ large bunch collard greens, tough ribs removed, triple-washed (page 18), and cut into strips (about 4 packed cups)

4 garlic cloves, finely chopped

Generous pinch of red pepper flakes

1½ cups heavy (whipping) cream

Juice of 1 lemon

Kosher salt and freshly ground black pepper

Freshly grated Parmesan cheese, for finishing

Extra-virgin olive oil, for finishing

In a large pot of salted boiling water, cook the pasta until al dente. Reserve 1 cup of the starchy pasta water and drain the pasta in a colander; set aside.

Return the pot to medium heat and cook the chopped bacon until golden. Transfer the crispy bacon to paper towels to drain. Add the collards to the hot bacon fat (they will spit as soon as they hit the fat). Once the sizzling subsides, return the pot to medium heat and sauté the collards until they turn bright green, about 1 minute. Toss in the garlic and red pepper flakes and stir for 30 seconds. Add the cream and lemon juice and simmer until the sauce thickens slightly, about 5 minutes. Season with salt and black pepper.

Turn off the heat. Add the pasta and reserved crispy bacon to the sauce along with about half of the reserved pasta water to loosen the sauce. Toss, toss, toss! Add more pasta water if needed. Cover the pot with a lid for 1 minute.

Divide the pasta among four warm bowls (see Tip, page 174).

Sprinkle with grated Parmesan, drizzle with extra-virgin olive oil, and dust with black pepper.

ROASTED CHICKEN POTPIE

Serves 6

Potpie is a Southern classic, but hasn't always been a favorite of mine. While most potpies are heavy with cream and butter, this one is packed with tender meat, vibrant vegetables, and crowned with a little white cheddar and bacon. This potpie isn't swimming in gravy, but instead, the gravy is served on the side, so people can have as much or as little as they like.

I usually make this dish over two days. On the first day, I make the pie dough and filling and store them in the fridge; the next day I assemble the pie and bake it.

For the pie dough:

2½ cups all-purpose flour

1 teaspoon kosher salt

2 sticks (8 ounces) cold unsalted butter, cubed

2 tablespoons bourbon (see Tip, page 241)

1 cup ice water

For the filling:

4 bone-in, skin-on chicken thighs (1½ pounds)

Kosher salt

2 tablespoons sunflower oil

2 slices thick-cut bacon, chopped

4 tablespoons unsalted butter

1 medium Yukon Gold potato, peeled and diced

2 medium carrots, peeled and finely chopped

MAKE THE PIE DOUGH:

In a stand mixer fitted with the flat beater attachment, combine the flour and salt with your fingertips. Add the cold butter and mix on a low speed until the dough looks like coarse sand. Turn the machine off and blend any large pieces of butter with your fingertips, making sure there are no pieces of butter larger than the size of a pea.

In a measuring cup, combine the bourbon and ice water. With the stand mixer on low, slowly dribble in the bourbon water 1 tablespoon at a time. Add just enough liquid for the dough to pull away from the sides of the bowl. (You may not need to use all the bourbon water.) Pinch the dough between your fingertips; it should be smooth, not sticky or crumbly. Gently press the dough together. Divide in half and shape each half into a disk. Wrap each disk in plastic wrap and refrigerate for at least 30 minutes or up to three days.

MAKE THE FILLING:

Preheat the oven to 425°F.

Lightly season both sides of the chicken with salt. Add the oil to a large 2- to 4-inch-deep cast iron skillet and set over medium-high heat. Once the oil is hot, add the chicken thighs, skin side down, and panfry until the skin is

**Leaves from 1 rosemary
sprig, finely chopped**

**½ teaspoon red pepper
flakes**

**1 medium yellow onion,
finely chopped**

**2 garlic cloves, finely
chopped**

**Freshly ground black
pepper**

**1 heaping tablespoon
all-purpose flour**

2 cups boiling water

¼ cup sour cream

For assembly:

Flour, for dusting

1 egg, for brushing

**¼ cup shredded white
cheddar cheese**

lightly golden and crispy, 8 to 10 minutes. Flip the thighs, transfer the skillet to the oven, and roast until the thighs are golden brown, about 25 minutes. Transfer the chicken to a plate to cool.

Place the same skillet over medium heat and cook the bacon until golden brown. Set aside the crispy bacon for assembly.

Add the butter to the pan drippings. Toss in the diced potato, carrots, rosemary, and red pepper flakes, making sure to scrape up any bits left over from the bacon. Cook the vegetables over medium heat for a few minutes, then toss in the onion and garlic. Season the vegetables with salt and pepper. Cook until the vegetables are slightly tender, about 5 to 8 minutes. (The vegetables will continue to cook in the oven later.)

Once the chicken is cool enough to handle, tear the chicken into bite-size pieces (discard the skin and bones). You should end up with 2 cups of chicken.

Add the chicken and flour to the vegetables. Add the boiling water and bring the filling to a boil. Once the mixture thickens slightly, take the skillet off the heat and add the sour cream. Season with salt and pepper. Drain into a large sieve set over a bowl to catch all the lovely gravy. (At this point you can store the filling and gravy in the fridge separately to use later, or allow the filling to cool completely if you are baking the pie the same day.)

ASSEMBLE AND BAKE THE POTPIE:

On a lightly floured surface, roll out 1 disk of dough, rotating in quarter-turns, until 12 to 14 inches in diameter and ⅛ inch thick. Gently fit the dough into a 9-inch pie plate. Trim the edges of the dough with scissors, making sure to leave at least a 1-inch overhang. (Reserve the scraps.)

(continued on page 183)

Crack the egg into a small dish. Without breaking the yolk, use a pastry brush to gently coat the bottom and sides of the pie shell with a thin layer of the egg white. The egg white creates a barrier between the filling and the crust as it bakes, keeping the crust from getting soggy. (Reserve the remaining egg for brushing the top crust.) Place the pie plate in the fridge while you roll out the rest of the dough.

Roll out the remaining disk of dough to a ⅛-inch thickness. Spoon the filling into the pie shell, topping with the reserved bacon and the cheddar. Gently place the top crust over the filling, trimming the edges with scissors so it is even with the bottom crust (reserve the scraps). Gently press to seal the edges of the pie dough so the top and bottom crusts stick to each other, then carefully roll the crust under itself so that the rolled edge sits on the "lip" of the pie plate. Crimp the edges. Beat the reserved egg and gently brush onto the edges and top of the pie.

Gather the reserved scraps of dough and roll out to the same thickness as the crust. With a sharp paring knife, cut out six leaf shapes. Place the leaves in a circular pattern on top of the potpie. (Each leaf represents a single portion of pie.) Gently brush the top of the leaves with the egg wash. Create vents disguised as "veins" in the leaves. The vents allow the steam to escape as it bakes. Place the pie in the fridge for 30 minutes to allow the pastry to set.

Meanwhile, preheat the oven to 425°F. Line a rimmed baking sheet with foil.

Place the pie on the lined baking sheet and bake the pie for 20 minutes. After 20 minutes, reduce the oven temperature to 375°F and bake until the crust is golden brown, about 30 minutes. Cover the edges with foil if they brown too quickly.

Let the pie cool for 5 to 10 minutes. Meanwhile, in a small saucepan, rewarm the gravy over medium-low heat.

Slice and serve with warm gravy on the side. Any leftover potpie will keep in the fridge, tightly wrapped, for three days.

VINEGAR CHICKEN WITH ALABAMA WHITE SAUCE

Serves 4

Vinegar is the crowning glory in this dish. The vinegar-soaked chicken finished off with a vinegary sauce may be excessive, and you'd be right. But there's nothing wrong with a little excess; as Mae West said, "Too much of a good thing can be wonderful." And that's what this dish is: mouthwatering, addictively tangy, and wonderful.

You can break down the chicken into four pieces or have your butcher do it for you. You will end up with two whole legs and two breasts with wings attached, which makes both dark and white meat lovers happy. Keep in mind that the chicken needs time to marinate before cooking, and you will need to get your hands on two cast iron skillets, one to cook the chicken in and another to act as a weight.

For the vinegar chicken:

2 cups distilled white vinegar

1 cup sunflower oil, plus more for frying

¼ cup kosher salt

1 teaspoon cayenne pepper

10 dashes of Tabasco chipotle pepper sauce

MAKE THE VINEGAR CHICKEN:

In a blender, combine the vinegar, 1 cup of the oil, salt, cayenne, chipotle pepper sauce, smoked paprika, black pepper, and garlic and blend until smooth. (Alternatively, you can use an immersion blender to blend the marinade.) Pour the marinade into a gallon-size plastic bag and toss in the chicken pieces. Marinate the chicken in the fridge for 12 hours.

Preheat the oven to 425°F.

Remove the chicken pieces from the marinade and pat them dry with paper towels.

1 tablespoon smoked
  sweet paprika
1 tablespoon freshly
  ground black pepper
4 garlic cloves, peeled
1 whole chicken (3½ to
  4 pounds), cut into
  4 pieces (2 whole breasts
  and 2 whole legs)

*For the Alabama
White Sauce:*
½ cup mayonnaise
¼ cup distilled white
  vinegar
1 teaspoon freshly
  ground black pepper

Pour ¼ inch of oil into a large ovenproof skillet and heat over medium-high heat. Once the oil is hot, arrange the chicken in the skillet, skin side down. The chicken should fit snugly in one layer. Loosely place a square of parchment on top of the chicken and weight the chicken down with a medium ovenproof skillet or heavy pot. Allow the chicken to cook under the weight of the skillet undisturbed for 20 minutes.

Take the skillet off the heat and carefully (it will be hot!) remove the top skillet (or heavy pot, if using). Flip the chicken, transfer the skillet to the oven, and roast until the thickest part of the thigh registers 165°F, 25 to 30 minutes.

MAKE THE ALABAMA WHITE SAUCE:

In a glass measuring cup, whisk together the mayonnaise, vinegar, and pepper. The white sauce should be thin and runny. Cover and refrigerate until ready to use. You can keep any leftover sauce in the fridge for one week.

Let the roasted chicken rest for 5 minutes. Arrange it on a platter. Spoon the sauce over the chicken and serve.

WHITE SAUCE AND THE WILSONS

Alabama White Sauce. I was introduced to this sauce at my in-laws' home. One of the first dinners at the Wilson house consisted of a lovely spread of vinegar-marinated barbecued chicken, baked potatoes, and a slew of sides. Bright Fiestaware plates adorned the table with pitchers of iced tea and lemonade at both ends. The chicken was a beautiful coral color, streaked by black grill marks. Steaming potatoes headed a procession of sides. Amid the colorful parade, I almost missed it. Tucked behind the iced tea pitcher was a little clear plastic container. The white sauce was flecked with cracked black pepper. My curiosity was piqued.

After saying the blessing, we all dug into the food and conversation. Moments later, Michael swiped the container of mystery sauce and shook it vigorously. With reckless abandon, he decanted the sauce over everything on his plate. The perky blue Fiestaware had snowy puddles flowing every which way. He passed the sauce to me. I poured a little ravine, innocently dividing my chicken and potatoes, a gorge that could be easily hidden in case I didn't like the mystery sauce. I eased a piece of chicken in and was pleasantly surprised. The sauce was deliciously tangy. Black pepper added a lovely contrast to this curious mayonnaise-based condiment. It was wonderful. I casually asked if this was a dressing of sorts. Conversation halted. Forks dropped. And I believe there was a cricket somewhere in the corner scratching away. It was as if I had asked if I could please take my pants off at the dinner table. Stunned faces stared at me, and Michael sweetly stated that it was Alabama White Sauce, not dressing. Utensils began to fly once more and before I knew it, dinner was over, and I could not help but think about this lovely pepper-speckled white sauce the Wilson family introduced me to. Alabama White Sauce to be exact.

CAJUN CHICKEN AND SAUSAGE GUMBO

Serves 6 to 8

Every household has picky eaters. My grandmother had a way of dealing with those who protested okra, bless their hearts. She would serve grandpa's Skillet-Fried Okra (page 133) on the side (instead of in the gumbo), and I follow by example. This is a great dish to make for entertaining: You should make it a day ahead—it is always better the next day. If you are lucky enough to have leftovers, spoon ¼ to ½ cup cold leftover rice into the bottom of a bowl, cover, and microwave for 30 seconds. Ladle rewarmed gumbo over the rice and serve.

---

3 bone-in, skin-on chicken thighs

Kosher salt

1 cup sunflower oil, plus more for coating the skillet

1 cup all-purpose flour

1 medium red onion, finely chopped

1 medium red bell pepper, finely chopped

6 garlic cloves, finely chopped

1 pound smoked sausage, cut into ½-inch-thick coins

Cayenne pepper

Pinch of red pepper flakes

(continued on page 191)

Preheat the oven to 425°F.

Lightly season the chicken with salt. Coat a medium cast iron or other heavy-bottomed skillet with oil and set over medium heat. Once the pan is hot, place the chicken thighs in the skillet, skin side down, and brown until the skin is lightly golden and crisp and the kitchen begins to fill with a nutty aroma, 8 to 10 minutes. (You know it's time to flip the thighs when the skin completely releases from the bottom of the skillet.) Flip the thighs, transfer the skillet to the oven, and roast until the thighs are golden brown, about 25 minutes. Set the chicken aside, reserving the drippings.

To make the roux, in a medium skillet heat the 1 cup oil over medium heat. Once hot, stir in the flour with a spoon or flat wooden spatula. The roux will immediately begin to thicken. Slowly stir the roux. At this point, you don't have to stir it constantly, but stay close to the stovetop and stir every minute or so. Once the roux turns the color of peanut butter, reduce the heat to medium-low. Slowly stir

8 cups hot water

**Freshly ground black
   pepper**

**Steamed Rice (page 28),
   for serving**

**Pepper Sauce (page 25),
   for serving**

constantly, making sure you scrape the bottom well. At this point, it's important to keep the roux moving in the skillet, closely watching it so it doesn't burn. (Burnt roux is distinctive; your kitchen will smell like burnt popcorn and the roux will turn black. If the roux burns, there's no saving it. Throw it out, chalk it up to experience, and confidently start again.) Once the roux turns the color of milk chocolate and smells deeply nutty, take the skillet off the heat and toss in the onion, bell pepper, and garlic. Stir until the sizzling subsides. (You can make the roux mixture a few hours ahead of time, storing in a glass measuring cup on the counter.)

Place a large heavy-bottomed pot over medium-high heat. Pour the golden drippings from the roasted chicken into the pot. Toss in the sausage and a pinch of cayenne pepper. Sear until the sausage caramelizes on both sides. Add the roasted chicken thighs, roux, red pepper flakes, and hot water. Season with salt, cayenne, and black pepper. Give the gumbo a good stir, making sure to scrape the bottom of the pot. Bring the gumbo to a boil, then reduce the heat to low. Place a lid on the pot slightly askew. (You want the gumbo to barely simmer. If you peek under the lid and the gumbo is steadily simmering, reduce the heat and add a few tablespoons of hot water to the pot.)

After 1 hour, remove the lid and skim any oil from the surface of the gumbo. Remove the chicken thighs. Shred the chicken with two forks (discard the skin and bones). Toss the shredded chicken back into the pot. Replace the lid, slightly askew, and continue slowly simmering the gumbo for 1 hour longer.

Take the gumbo off the heat and skim the surface of any oil. Adjust the salt, cayenne, and black pepper to taste. Spoon ¼ to ½ cup rice into each bowl, ladle the gumbo over the rice, and serve with pepper sauce.

ROASTED NASHVILLE HOT CHICKEN

Serves 4

When I moved to Nashville, I was immediately introduced to the local favorite dish, hot chicken. Hot chicken is fried in a cast iron skillet and tossed in a reddish cayenne paste, then served with pickles and white bread, which gets soaked through with shockingly spicy orange chicken drippings.

Although traditionally Nashville hot chicken is fried then tossed in a hot chicken paste, I prefer the method of quickly pan-frying the thighs on the stovetop, then roasting them in the oven. The result is crispy skin and juicy dark meat. While the chicken finishes off in the oven, I have time to clean up the kitchen and get ready for company.

---

8 bone-in, skin-on chicken thighs

Kosher salt

2 tablespoons sunflower oil

½ cup olive oil

2 tablespoons cayenne pepper

1 tablespoon dark brown sugar

½ teaspoon smoked sweet paprika

½ teaspoon chili powder

Preheat the oven to 425°F.

Use paper towels to gently blot the chicken thighs, removing the moisture from the surface of the chicken. This will ensure you get a nice crisp skin. Lightly season both sides with salt.

In a large cast iron or ovenproof skillet, heat the sunflower oil over medium heat. Once the oil is hot, gently place the chicken thighs in the pan, skin side down, and panfry until the skin is golden and crisp, 8 to 10 minutes. (You know it's time to flip the thighs when the skin completely releases from the bottom of the skillet.) Flip the thighs, immediately transfer the skillet to the oven, and roast until the thighs are golden brown and the internal temperature is 165°F, 25 to 30 minutes.

In a small bowl, whisk together the olive oil, cayenne, brown sugar, smoked paprika, chili powder, and 2 teaspoons salt.

While the chicken is still piping hot, brush the chicken with the paste. Serve straight from the skillet.

CHICKEN AND SAUSAGE JAMBALAYA

Serves 6 to 8

Tabasco chipotle pepper sauce is my favorite condiment to serve alongside jambalaya. It adds just the right amount of smokiness and spice to the finished dish. Also, I've found the best way to reheat single portions of the leftovers is to place a damp paper towel over the bowl before microwaving. (The damp paper towel keeps the rice from drying out as it reheats.)

6 bone-in, skin-on chicken thighs, at room temperature

Kosher salt

2 tablespoons sunflower oil

1 pound smoked sausage, cubed

2 tablespoons unsalted butter

1 medium yellow onion, finely chopped

2 red bell peppers, finely chopped

2 serrano peppers, seeded and finely chopped

1 bunch green onions (scallions), white and pale green parts only, thinly sliced

3 celery stalks, finely chopped

(continued on page 197)

Preheat the oven to 425°F.

Lightly season the chicken thighs with salt. In a large ovenproof skillet, heat the oil over medium heat. Once the oil is hot, add the chicken thighs, skin side down. Cook until the skin is golden brown, 8 to 10 minutes. Flip the thighs, transfer the skillet to the oven, and roast until the thighs are golden brown, about 25 minutes.

Reserving the drippings in the pan, transfer the chicken to a plate to cool. Use the tines of a fork to pull the skin off the chicken thighs (discard the skin). When the thighs are cool enough to handle, hand-tear the chicken (discard the bones). Set aside on a plate.

Pour the chicken drippings into a large heavy-bottomed pot over medium heat. Add the sausage and sear until it carmelizes, 8 to 10 minutes. With a slotted spoon, transfer the sausage to the plate with the chicken.

Add the butter to the pot. Once the butter melts, add the yellow onion and cook until it softens, about 5 minutes. Toss in the bell peppers, serranos, green onions, celery, garlic, 1 tablespoon salt, black pepper, cayenne, smoked paprika, chili powder, oregano, and tomato paste. Add 1 cup of the hot water and stir, scraping the bottom of the pot. Once the water evaporates and the vegetables begin

4 garlic cloves, finely
  chopped
1 teaspoon freshly ground
  black pepper
½ teaspoon cayenne
  pepper
¼ teaspoon smoked sweet
  paprika
¼ teaspoon chili powder
Leaves from 2 oregano
  sprigs, finely chopped
2 tablespoons tomato
  paste
2 cups hot water, plus
  more if needed
2 cups long-grain rice
Parsley leaves, for serving
Tabasco chipotle pepper
  sauce, for serving

sticking to the bottom of the pot, about 5 minutes, add the chicken, sausage, and remaining 1 cup hot water. Allow the water to evaporate again, about 5 minutes.

While the water is evaporating, toss the rice into a sieve and rinse with cold water until the water runs clear.

Add the rinsed rice and 2½ cups cold water to the pot. Cover with a lid and return to low heat, and cook until the rice is tender, not mushy or crunchy, 30 to 40 minutes. While the jambalaya cooks, check it occasionally and give it a good stir. (The jambalaya should be steadily simmering away.) If the rice is sticking to the bottom of the pot, pour in a tablespoon of hot water and scrape the bottom. Replace the lid and continue cooking.

Remove the pot from the heat and let sit, covered, for 10 minutes. Stir well and taste the jambalaya, adjusting seasoning if necessary and checking to be sure the rice is cooked through. (If the rice has cooked unevenly, put the lid back on the pot for another 10 minutes and check it again.) Transfer to a serving dish and sprinkle with parsley and serve with chipotle pepper sauce on the side.

DESSERTS

WATERMELON AND SEA SALT

During the summer, when watermelons are at their peak, I remember my grandmother retrieving a large tray of ice-cold watermelon straight from the fridge in the garage after dinner. She plopped the tray of ruby slices of melon on the picnic table in her backyard and pulled out the little glass salt shaker that was cleverly tucked away in her back pocket. She taught me to add a little salt to each slice of cold watermelon. The salt complements the delicious flavor of the melon. It made for the simplest summertime dessert.

There are a few tips for picking out a flavorful watermelon. Look for a melon with a yellow belly. The yellow "belly" is the spot where the watermelon has been sitting in the field. If the belly is pale or nonexistent, this means the melon was picked too early. The melon should be heavy, meaning it's ripe and full of juice. The last tip is to knock on the melon. The sound should be full, not dull.

---

1 medium watermelon
Fine sea salt

Cut the melon into wedges, chunks, or spears. Chill until ready to serve. Just before serving, sprinkle each piece of melon with sea salt.

HONEY-ROASTED PEACH "BUTTERMILK" ICE CREAM

Makes 1½ quarts

Notice this recipe does not call for buttermilk. The combination of lemon-soaked peaches churned with the creamy ice cream base creates a wonderfully tangy buttermilk flavor, which also cuts the sweetness of the ice cream.

1½ pounds peaches, halved and pitted

3 tablespoons honey

Juice of ½ lemon

2 cups milk

2 cups sugar

Pinch of kosher salt

1 vanilla bean, split lengthwise

2 cups heavy (whipping) cream

Preheat the oven to 425°F. Line a rimmed baking sheet with parchment paper.

In a medium bowl, toss together the peaches, 2 tablespoons of the honey, and the lemon juice. Arrange the peach halves cut side up on the lined baking sheet and roast until the peaches caramelize and soften, about 30 minutes.

Puree the peach flesh and skin in a blender until smooth. Place the peach puree in an airtight container and stash in the fridge.

In a medium saucepan, combine the milk and sugar. Whisk over medium heat until the sugar completely dissolves and tiny bubbles form around the edges of the pan. Take off the heat and whisk in the salt. Scrape in the vanilla seeds and add the vanilla pod. Let steep and cool for 10 minutes. Whisk in the heavy cream. Cover and refrigerate for 4 to 8 hours.

Discard the vanilla pod and transfer the chilled ice cream base to an ice cream maker. Churn according to the manufacturer's instructions. Once the mixture thickens, add the pureed peaches, 1 tablespoon at a time, and the remaining 1 tablespoon honey while the ice cream maker churns. Once the machine has finished churning, scoop the ice cream into a freezerproof container and freeze for at least 2 hours before serving.

BLACKBERRY AND HONEY ICE CREAM

Serves 6

This is a simple ice cream recipe to keep in your back pocket. Blackberry and honey is one of my favorite combinations, but you can substitute strawberries, dark cherries, raspberries, or blueberries for the blackberries, if you prefer.

---

1 cup whole milk

1 cup sugar

Pinch of kosher salt

1 vanilla bean, split
  lengthwise

1 cup heavy (whipping)
  cream

½ cup blackberries, larger
  berries halved

1 tablespoon honey

In a small saucepan, combine the milk and sugar. Stir over medium heat until the sugar completely dissolves. Take the saucepan off the heat and add the salt. Scrape in the vanilla seeds and add the vanilla pod. Let steep in the milk for 10 minutes. Whisk in the heavy cream. Transfer to an airtight container and refrigerate for 3 to 4 hours, until the ice cream base is completely chilled.

Discard the vanilla pod and transfer the chilled ice cream base to an ice cream maker. Churn according to the manufacturer's instructions. Once the mixture thickens, add the blackberries and drizzle in the honey while the ice cream maker churns. Once the machine has finished churning, scoop the ice cream into a freezerproof container and freeze for at least 2 hours before serving.

VARIATIONS

Mint Ice Cream: Substitute ½ cup roughly chopped fresh mint for the blackberries and honey. Add the mint to the ice cream base when you add the vanilla seeds and pod and let steep as directed. If you want a deep mint flavor, leave the mint leaves in the ice cream; if you want a subtle mint flavor, strain and discard the mint right before adding the chilled ice cream base to the ice cream maker.

Sea Salt Caramel Ice Cream: Substitute ½ cup chilled Sea Salt Caramel (page 60) for the blackberries and honey. Drizzle in the chilled caramel after scooping the ice cream into a freezer-proof container. With a spoon gently ripple the caramel so you can see amber streaks of caramel against the pale cream; freeze for at least two hours before serving.

MELTING SUMMER DAYS

For several years, my family had an end-of-summer getaway on the Gulf of Mexico, at the vacation house of family friends. They had a summer home, which made them the most lavish people we knew. It didn't matter that there were wheelbarrows lining the stairway to the house, that the kitchen had chipped linoleum floors, and that there was no air conditioning. Honestly, it was one step away from camping, but as a child I didn't notice. It was a summer home.

Our alarm clock each morning was a large, wooden ice cream maker churning away underneath the raised home. (The house was elevated on stilts about fifteen feet above ground to protect it from rising waters during hurricane season.) The men started churning the ice cream early in the day while sipping on their coffees. Us kids always made it down in time to toss in handfuls of freshly picked berries before the aluminum cylinder was covered and safely stored away in a deep freeze for later.

We spent our days collecting oysters. We tossed the oysters into a galvanized bucket, and once the pail was filled to the brim, we brought it to a picnic table that was perfectly perched at the end of the dock. One of the older boys took a small, sharp knife and slowly pried the shell open, jiggled the oyster free, and handed it to me. The oyster slid to the back of my throat like a sweet yet salty egg yolk.

Roped to the dock were a dozen or so crab traps. We gently lifted the traps and carried any unfortunate captives upstairs to the kitchen, being careful not to trample the honey-scented gardenia bushes that lined the staircase. The women prepared all the trimmings while the men gathered the propane tanks and large silver pots outside. In no time the salty summer air burst with Cajun spices, and we sat down to a great boil.

As the sun began to set, the scent of spices became a faint memory. The aluminum cylinder was raised from the depths of the deep freeze, and we began scooping out servings of thick, creamy ice cream. We sat on top of the wooden picnic table at the end of the dock, kicking our feet, watching our reflections on the water. I placed my hand on the table, tracing the initials I had carved into the weathered wood, making sure I treasured this moment as my childhood summer days started melting away, fading faster than ice cream in August.

CANE SYRUP CARAMELS

Makes 32 pieces

To most Southerners, it's as important to leave with your arms full of food as it is a full tummy. It's Southern hospitality concealed in humble foil, brown paper, and plastic bags. I've adopted a similar tradition: As guests leave I hand them sweet treats—more often than not a cellophane bag filled with these caramels.

Sunflower oil

1½ cups sugar

¼ cup light corn syrup

1 cup heavy (whipping) cream

5 tablespoons unsalted butter

1 teaspoon sea salt, plus more for sprinkling

1 tablespoon cane syrup

1 tablespoon vanilla extract

Line an 8 x 8-inch baking pan with parchment paper with excess hanging over the edges of the pan. (The excess parchment will act as your handle to get the caramels out of the pan later.) Dab a paper towel with some oil and rub it on the parchment paper, including up the sides. Set the pan aside.

In a medium saucepan, stir together the sugar, corn syrup, and ¼ cup water. Bring to a boil over medium-high heat and continue to boil until the sugar turns amber in color, about 10 minutes.

Meanwhile, in a small saucepan, heat the cream, butter, and sea salt until the mixture comes to a simmer. Remove from the heat and add the cane syrup and vanilla.

When the sugar–corn syrup mixture turns amber, take it off the heat and slowly add the cream mixture. Be careful because the mixture will bubble up violently. (Keep your arms and hands away from the steam.) Put the saucepan over medium heat and cook the caramel until a candy thermometer registers 245° to 248°F (the firm ball stage). Take the saucepan off the heat and pour it into the prepared baking pan lined with parchment paper. Refrigerate the caramel until it cools completely, about 1 hour.

Once cool, use the parchment paper overhang to remove the caramel from the pan and sprinkle with sea salt. Slice the caramel into 32 rectangular pieces. Wrap each caramel in a piece of parchment paper or a candy wrapper, and refrigerate until ready to enjoy. These caramels can also be frozen for up to six months.

BACON BOURBON BRITTLE

Serves 8

Have all the ingredients on hand before you start making this candy. This brittle will demand your undivided attention, and it is not forgiving if you are trying to measure out baking soda or fry bacon once you start making the candy. Trust me. If you take your eye off the brittle, it can quickly turn hard as a rock and could crack your teeth. This brittle can be stored in an airtight container at room temperature, layered between pieces of parchment paper, for one week. Save the bacon fat in a jar in the fridge for the next time you sauté greens or fry eggs.

Sunflower oil, for greasing parchment paper

1 cup sugar

½ cup light corn syrup

2 tablespoons unsalted butter

Scant 1 teaspoon baking soda

2 tablespoons bourbon

1 cup roughly chopped crisp-cooked bacon

Line a large rimmed baking sheet with parchment paper and brush with oil.

In a small saucepan, bring the sugar, corn syrup, and 3 tablespoons water to a boil over medium heat. Fit the saucepan with a candy thermometer and cook until the thermometer registers 290°F.

Add the butter and stir often until the thermometer reads 300°F. Take the saucepan off the heat and add the baking soda, bourbon, and bacon. Stir together and immediately pour onto the prepared baking sheet and spread with a heatproof spatula. Let cool completely and break into pieces.

PECAN, FIG, AND HONEY DIVINITY

Makes 32 pieces

Divinity is Southern nougat. I make double and triple batches of divinity around the holidays, while satsumas are in season, to give away as gifts. I wrap them in clear cellophane, showing off the pecans and figs.

Sunflower oil, for greasing pan

1½ cups granulated sugar

¼ cup light corn syrup

⅓ cup honey

2 egg whites, at room temperature

Pinch of kosher salt

1 tablespoon vanilla extract

1 teaspoon grated satsuma or orange zest

½ cup pecan halves, toasted (see Tip, page 216) and roughly chopped

1 cup dried figs, stemmed and roughly chopped

Powdered sugar, for dusting

Line an 8 x 8-inch baking pan with parchment paper with excess hanging over the edges of the pan. (The excess parchment will act as your handle to help get the nougat out of the pan later.) Dab a paper towel with oil and rub it onto the parchment paper, including up the sides. Cut a square of parchment paper slightly larger than the baking pan, rub it with oil, and set aside. (This piece will be used to place on top of the divinity once the candy is in the pan.)

In a small saucepan over high heat, combine the granulated sugar, corn syrup, honey, and 1 cup water. Attach a candy thermometer to the side of the saucepan and cook the syrup until it reaches 300°F.

Meanwhile, in a stand mixer fitted with the whisk attachment, whisk the egg whites and salt on medium speed until soft peaks form.

When the syrup reaches 300°F, slowly pour the hot syrup into the whipped egg whites with the machine running on low. Once the syrup is completely combined, increase the speed to high and keep whisking for 10 minutes, or until very thick. Stop the machine and add the vanilla and satsuma zest. Continue whipping for 30 seconds. With a rubber spatula, quickly fold in the pecans and figs and immediately transfer the mixture to the prepared baking pan. Place the remaining piece of greased parchment paper on top (oil side down). Press down, coaxing the mixture into the corners, and smooth the top of the divinity with your hands. Refrigerate for at least eight hours.

(continued on following page)

Dust a cutting board with powdered sugar. Remove the top piece of parchment and unmold the divinity onto the board. Remove and discard the bottom parchment paper. Run a large knife under piping hot water and wipe dry. Cut the divinity into 4 equal strips. Then cut each strip crosswise into 8 equal pieces for a total of 32 pieces. Dust more powdered sugar onto the work surface and onto the divinity. (Keep in mind this is a soft candy, so it will be on the sticky side. I keep a fine-mesh sieve filled with powdered sugar at hand to dust the candy as needed.) Roll up each piece in a wax or a glassine candy wrapper and store in the fridge for up to three days.

Tip: To toast the pecans, simply place the pecans on a small baking sheet and bake for 8 minutes in a 350°F oven.

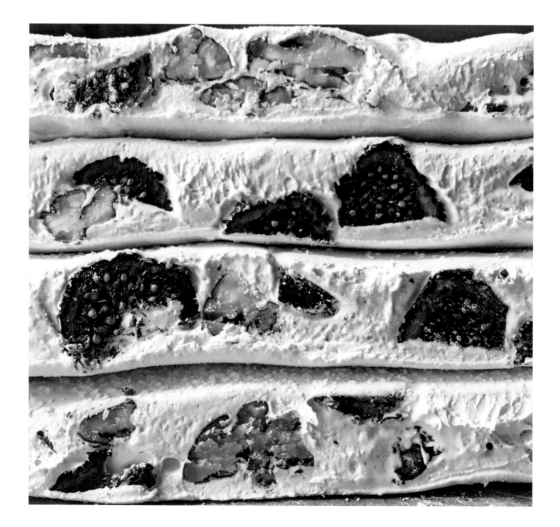

PECAN DIVINITY

As my husband and I drove down the long, dusty road, I noticed a few fields of Alabama cotton that had yet to be cleared. We slowly crept to a halt as we got to the end of the road and inched over a set of railroad tracks. As we passed over the tracks, it was as if we went back in time—a time when Southern traditions were worn like a strand of cherished pearls: donned daily around the neck and treasured close to the heart.

Mighty magnolias and precious pecan trees covered the grounds of the estate. The owner had graciously extended an invitation to pick pecans on her lovely grounds. Branches bowed as if they were kindly welcoming our arrival. Pecan trees were freckled with pecan fruits in their bright green husks, which harbored tiger-striped shells just waiting to drop to the ground. I gathered as many pecans that had already fallen as I could before the squirrels could get their greedy paws on them.

With my basket filled to the brim with pecans, I made my way into the old house. The worn wooden floors whispered and groaned as if they could tell tales of the children who grew up in these corridors. Those children have grown and now have their own children scurrying about the house, writing new chapters into the history and halls of the estate.

In front of an enormous fireplace in the main living room stood two matching wingback chairs angled toward each other with a table nestled in between. On top of the wooden table rested a crystal bottle filled with brandy and two digestif glasses placed in front of the bottle. This setting tells an unspoken story of two people taking time at the end of the evening, relaxing in front of the crackling fire, enjoying something to drink that warmed their bodies and spirits. This simple setting taught me something about the past. The past does not have to only live in photos on the wall or in worn floorboards, but it can also be kept alive in small, tangible daily rituals. I watched the magnolias fade into the distance as we passed over the tracks once again. I sat there with my basket filled with pecans and couldn't help but think about the importance of daily rituals in our everyday lives. Here is to restoring old traditions and creating new ones that will live on in our spirits and homes for generations to come.

BOURBON MARSHMALLOWS

Makes 16 large or 32 small marshmallows

Serve these wonderfully springy marshmallows with your favorite hot chocolate, sandwiched in between chocolate and graham crackers for luscious s'mores, or packaged in cellophane bags as gifts for guests to bring home and indulge in after a dinner party. The marshmallows will be set after four hours, but if you want to make these the night before and cut them in the morning, they will keep just fine on the countertop.

Sunflower oil, for greasing
   pan
¼ cup bourbon, chilled
Seeds of 1 vanilla bean
3 envelopes (¼ ounce
   each) unflavored gelatin
2 cups granulated sugar
⅔ cup light corn syrup
¼ teaspoon kosher salt
½ cup powdered sugar

Line an 8 x 8-inch baking pan with parchment paper with excess hanging over the edges of the pan. (The excess parchment will act as your handle to get the marshmallows out of the pan later.) Dab a paper towel with oil and rub it onto the parchment paper, including up the sides. Set the pan aside.

In the bowl of a stand mixer fitted with the whisk attachment, use a spoon to lightly stir the cold bourbon, vanilla seeds, ¼ cup cold water, and the gelatin. Let stand until the gelatin softens and absorbs liquid, at least 15 minutes.

In a medium saucepan, combine the granulated sugar, corn syrup, salt, and ½ cup cold water. (This size pan is necessary as the syrup bubbles up quite a lot as it cooks!) Stir over medium heat until the sugar dissolves. Attach a candy thermometer to the side of the pan and boil, without stirring, until the syrup reaches 240°F, about 8 minutes.

With the mixer on low speed, slowly pour the hot syrup into the gelatin mixture in a thin stream down the side of the bowl. Gradually increase the speed to high and whisk until the mixture is thick and stiff, about 15 minutes.

Quickly scrape the mixture into the prepared pan. Smooth the top with a wet offset spatula. Let stand uncovered at room temperature for at least 4 hours and up to 8 hours.

Sift a generous dusting of powdered sugar onto a work surface, forming a square slightly larger than your pan. Turn the marshmallow slab onto the work surface and peel the parchment off the slab. Sift more powdered sugar over the top of the marshmallow.

Cut the slab in 4 long equal pieces. Cut each strip crosswise into 4 equal pieces. You will end up with 16 square marshmallows. These are perfect for s'mores! If you cut each square in half again, you will end up with 32 rectangular marshmallows, which are lovely for desserts, to serve in cider or hot chocolate, or to give away as gifts.

Toss the marshmallows in the powdered sugar to coat and shake off any excess. Store in an airtight container at room temperature for up to two weeks.

GINGER AND CANE SYRUP COOKIES

Makes 24 cookies

Keep in mind this dough is best made a day before you bake the cookies—it allows the flavors to marry—but if you're in a rush, thirty minutes will do the trick! Also, this dough freezes beautifully (see Tip, page 225) making it great to have on hand in case you have unexpected guests or an emergency cookie craving.

2¾ cups all-purpose flour

1 teaspoon baking soda

¾ teaspoon kosher salt

2½ teaspoons ground ginger

1½ teaspoons ground cinnamon

¼ teaspoon ground cloves

Grated zest of 2 medium satsumas or 1 orange (about 2 teaspoons)

Seeds of 1 vanilla bean

¾ cup packed dark brown sugar

1½ sticks (6 ounces) unsalted butter, at room temperature

¾ cup cane syrup

1 large egg, at room temperature

¼ cup raw cane sugar, plus more if needed, for coating

In a small bowl, whisk together the flour, baking soda, salt, ginger, cinnamon, and cloves and set aside.

In a stand mixer fitted with the flat beater attachment, combine the satsuma zest, vanilla seeds, brown sugar, and butter and beat on low, gradually increasing the speed to medium. Beat for 5 minutes, scrape down the bowl, and beat for 5 minutes more.

(Alternatively, you can use a hand mixer. Just keep in mind that it takes 10 minutes to cream the butter and sugar.)

Put the cane syrup in a glass measuring cup and crack the egg into it. Whisk with a fork until just combined. Scrape the bowl of the stand mixer. With the mixer on medium speed, pour in the syrup-egg mixture. Beat for 1 minute, then reduce the speed to low. Slowly add the flour mixture. Once the flour is incorporated, scrape down the bowl, making sure there aren't any bits of flour hiding at the bottom of the bowl. Transfer the dough to an airtight container and refrigerate for at least 30 minutes or up to 24 hours. (You can skip chilling the dough and freeze it at this point for later; see Tip, page 225.)

Preheat the oven to 350°F. Line two large rimmed baking sheets with parchment paper.

(continued on page 225)

Coat the bottom of a shallow dish with the cane sugar. Using a 1½-tablespoon cookie dough scoop (or a tablespoon), portion the dough into 24 balls. Roll each piece in between your palms, creating a smooth ball of dough.

Roll each ball in the raw cane sugar, making sure it is evenly coated, and place on the prepared baking sheets, spacing them 2 inches apart, as they spread while baking.

Bake until the tops are lovely and cracked and the edges are golden, 10 to 15 minutes. Let cool on the baking sheet for 1 to 2 minutes, then transfer to a wire rack to cool completely. These cookies can be stored for up to three days in an airtight container at room temperature.

Tip: To freeze the dough, halve the prepared dough and wrap each piece in parchment paper. Fold the edges tightly and create a log shape, twisting the ends together until the log resembles a Christmas cracker. Place the logs in a freezer bag, label the bag, and store in the freezer for up to three months. Thaw for at least 8 hours in the fridge before baking. When ready to bake, portion each log into 12 equal slices and shape these slices into balls. Roll in sugar and bake as directed.

GRAPEFRUIT ANGEL WINGS

Makes 35 to 40 pieces

These buttery, sugar-covered fried treats are traditionally eaten during Carnival season right before the season of Lent. But honestly, I love to serve them all year to keep the spirit of Mardi Gras alive. Also, you can substitute lemon, lime, or orange zest for the grapefruit zest.

½ cup granulated sugar

Grated zest of 1 medium grapefruit (about 1 tablespoon)

2 cups all-purpose flour, plus more for dusting

¾ teaspoon kosher salt

½ teaspoon baking powder

6 tablespoons unsalted butter, cubed, at room temperature

3 large eggs, at room temperature

2 tablespoons vanilla extract

Peanut oil, for frying

1 cup Superfine Vanilla Sugar (page 28), for coating

In a small bowl, combine the granulated sugar and grapefruit zest. Rub the zest into the sugar with your fingertips.

In a stand mixer fitted with the flat beater attachment, combine the flour, salt, and baking powder with your fingers. Create a well in the center and add the butter, eggs, vanilla, and zest-sugar mixture. Mix on low until the ingredients are combined and begin to form a soft dough, about 2 minutes. Shape the dough into a ball, cover it in plastic wrap, and refrigerate for 2 hours.

Between two pieces of parchment paper, roll the dough to a ¼-inch thickness. (If the dough is thicker than ¼ inch, the angel wings will puff up too much while frying, and they will end up heavy and cakelike instead of delicate and crisp.) Cut the dough into 2-inch-wide strips. Cut again on a diagonal, creating diamond-shaped pieces. The dough is very delicate, so be as gentle as possible.

In a large cast iron skillet, heat 2 inches of peanut oil over medium heat to 325°F. Line a plate with paper towels. Fill a shallow bowl with the vanilla sugar.

Working in batches, gently place the pieces of dough into the oil, and fry until they get beautifully golden on both sides, 2 to 3 minutes total. Drain on the paper towels, then toss in the vanilla sugar. Devour immediately. If by some miracle you have leftovers, just seal them up in a plastic bag, keep them at room temperature, *et voilà*! Breakfast is ready for you in the morning.

THE PRODIGIOUS GRAPEFRUIT

I'm seven years old, riding down the long, dusty road to Lacassine, Louisiana. Cleared sugarcane fields reveal new life from the rich soil, and a sweet fragrance fills the warm air. I imagine the empty field in late summer, taking over the scenery with its towering foliage. I become entranced by the pale jade landscape as we creep closer and closer to my great-grandma's house.

I tiptoe across the tiny white shells in my great-grandmother's driveway, go around the corner of her small whitewashed house, and step into the garden. To me, this is an enchanted backyard, filled with life from one end of the tiny lot to the other. Vibrant red and green peppers pirouette in the breeze, reminding me of flickering Christmas lights. A fig tree magically becomes the perfect umbrella to take refuge under amid afternoon showers. Near the back of the property, there is a gaggle of chickens that become disgruntled if you get too close to their coop.

I decide to keep my distance from the foul fowls and keep to the side of the house, close to my grandmother, who is reaching over her head, picking what look like spotted yellow basketballs. Quietly but curiously, I begin filling as many plastic shopping bags with the fruit as I can and pile them into the back seat of the car. The combination of the sweet air from the sugarcane fields and the fresh scent of the mysterious citrus resting on my lap makes my mouth water.

When we get back to the house, my grandma grabs a large carving knife and splits the colossal citrus in half, revealing blushing pink flesh. My grandma smiles proudly and says in her sweet Cajun accent, "Dat's a biiggg grapefruit!" My mouth drops open in sheer disbelief, and we both start laughing and begin ripping into the slightly sweet and tart flesh.

With a mouthful of ruby grapefruit and pink juice dribbling down my chin, I wonder what the secret is to the gigantic, sugary grapefruits that grew in my great-grandmother's backyard. I recall the soft breeze coming from the sugarcane field across the way and become sweetly satisfied in being naïve of the mystery behind the prodigious grapefruit.

CHICORY COFFEE MERINGUES

Makes 6 meringues

These are my favorite kind of meringues: crispy on the outside and marshmallow-y on the inside. I do recommend making these the day of or the day before serving them, especially if you live in an area with constant high humidity levels, like I do. The meringues tend to get a little tacky if left out on my countertop any longer than a few days.

3 large egg whites, at
　room temperature
½ cup Superfine Vanilla
　Sugar (page 28)
Pinch of kosher salt
1½ teaspoons cornstarch
1 teaspoon distilled white
　vinegar
1 teaspoon finely ground
　chicory coffee

Preheat the oven to 200°F. Fit a large rimmed baking sheet with a wire rack. Line the rack with parchment paper, folding the excess parchment underneath the rack so it doesn't shift around.

Fill a small saucepan halfway with water and bring to a simmer over medium-low heat.

In a stand mixer fitted with the whisk attachment, whip the egg whites on medium-low speed until foamy. Add the vanilla sugar, salt, cornstarch, and vinegar. Whisk until just combined.

Place the mixer bowl over the simmering water and slowly stir the meringue mixture for 2 to 3 minutes with a rubber spatula. The mixture should feel completely smooth between your fingertips; if it is grainy, continue mixing.

Return the bowl to the stand mixer and continue whisking until stiff peaks form.

Spoon 6 medium mounds of meringue onto the parchment paper. Sprinkle each mound with the chicory coffee. With a teaspoon, shape the meringues, starting from the base and sweeping around and up to the top, creating a small peak.

Place the meringues in the oven for 3 hours. Turn off the oven and allow the meringues to completely dry in the oven for an hour or so, or until they are stiff and no longer sticky.

Place the meringues in an airtight container until you are ready to serve them. (Be careful not to let the meringues touch once they are stored.) These meringues will keep in an airtight container on the countertop for 1 to 2 days.

BLACKBERRY CAKE

Makes 12 servings

Since this is an all-butter cake, it is best served warm, straight out of the oven. If there are leftovers, wrap them up as soon as possible, as this cake will become dry if left out too long. Any leftovers can be reheated and served with your morning coffee for a lovely, delicious breakfast.

8 tablespoons (1 stick) unsalted butter, at room temperature, plus more for greasing pan

All-purpose flour, for dusting pan

½ cup granulated sugar

¼ cup Superfine Vanilla Sugar (page 28)

2 large eggs, at room temperature

½ cup whole milk

1 teaspoon vanilla extract

Pinch of kosher salt

1½ cups self-rising flour, sifted

1 cup fresh or frozen blackberries

Powdered sugar, for dusting

Preheat the oven to 325°F. Grease and flour a 10-cup Bundt pan, shaking out any excess flour.

In a stand mixer fitted with the whisk attachment, cream the butter, granulated sugar, and vanilla sugar together for 5 minutes on medium. Scrape the bowl down and continue whisking for another 5 minutes. (Alternatively, you can use a hand mixer. Just keep in mind that it takes 10 minutes to cream the butter and sugar.)

Add the eggs one at a time, beating well after each addition. Slowly add the milk and vanilla and whisk for a few more minutes. The batter will resemble cottage cheese and you will think you've ruined the batter. Add the salt, then add the flour, 1 tablespoon at a time. Watch the lumpy batter transform to a smooth, airy batter.

Once all the flour is incorporated fold in half of the blackberries. Pour the batter into the prepared pan. Even out the top of the batter. Sprinkle the remaining blackberries over the top, gently pressing the berries into the batter. Bake until the top is golden brown and a toothpick inserted in the center comes out clean, 45 minutes to 1 hour.

Let the cake cool in the pan on a wire rack for 5 to 10 minutes. Invert the cake onto a serving plate. Dust with powdered sugar and serve warm.

LOVELY BLACKBERRY PIE

Makes one 9-inch pie

This is my version of Grandma and Grandpa's blackberry pie (photograph on page 198). Be sure to give yourself time to allow the blackberry filling to cool completely before assembling the pie. If you are in a rush, simply spread the filling out in the largest glass baking dish you have and place in the fridge before making the pie dough.

For the pie dough:

2½ cups all-purpose flour, plus more for dusting

1 teaspoon kosher salt

3 tablespoons sugar

2 sticks (8 ounces) cold unsalted butter, cubed

2 tablespoons bourbon (see Tip, page 241)

1 cup ice water

For the filling:

1 pound fresh or frozen blackberries

¾ cup sugar

3 tablespoons cornstarch

1 teaspoon vanilla extract

¼ teaspoon ground cinnamon

Juice of 1 lemon

For assembly:

1 egg, for brushing

1 tablespoon sugar, for sprinkling

MAKE THE PIE DOUGH:

In a stand mixer fitted with the flat beater attachment, combine the flour, salt, and sugar with your fingertips. Add the cold butter and mix on a low speed until the dough looks like coarse sand. Turn the machine off and blend any large pieces of butter with your fingertips, making sure there are no pieces of butter larger than the size of a pea.

In a measuring cup, combine the bourbon and ice water. With the stand mixer on a low speed, slowly dribble in the bourbon 1 tablespoon at a time. Add just enough liquid for the dough to pull away from the sides of the bowl. (You may not need to use all the bourbon water.) Pinch the dough between your fingertips; it should be smooth, not sticky or crumbly. Gently press the dough together. Divide in half and shape each half into a disk. Wrap each disk in plastic wrap and refrigerate for at least 30 minutes or up to 3 days.

MAKE THE FILLING:

In a medium saucepan, stir together the blackberries, sugar, cornstarch, vanilla, cinnamon, half of the lemon juice, and 2 tablespoons water. Bring to a boil over medium-high heat, then reduce to a simmer and cook, stirring occasionally, until thick enough to coat the back of a spoon, 20 to 25 minutes. Remove from the heat and stir in the remaining lemon juice. Let the filling cool slightly, then transfer to an airtight container and refrigerate to cool completely before assembling the pie.

ASSEMBLE AND BAKE THE PIE:

On a lightly floured surface, roll out 1 disk of dough, rotating it in quarter-turns, until 12 to 14 inches in diameter and ⅛ inch thick. Gently fit the dough into a 9-inch pie plate. Trim the edges of the dough with scissors, making sure to leave a 1-inch overhang.

Crack the egg into a small dish. Without breaking the yolk, use a pastry brush to gently coat the bottom and sides of the pie shell with a thin layer of the egg white. The egg white creates a barrier between the filling and the crust as it bakes, keeping the crust from getting soggy. (Reserve the remaining egg for brushing the top crust.) Place the pie shell in the fridge for 30 minutes.

Meanwhile, roll out the remaining disk of dough, rotating it in quarter-turns, to a ⅛-inch thickness. Cut the dough into six 1½-inch-wide strips. (I use a fluted pastry cutter to get those beautiful old-fashioned edges.) Place the strips on a rimmed baking sheet and set aside in the fridge until ready to assemble.

Pour the cooled filling into the chilled pie shell. Place 3 strips of dough on top of the filling horizontally. Then, one by one, place the remaining 3 strips vertically, lifting every other horizontal strip to create a basket weave lattice. Trim the edges with scissors even with the bottom crust. Gently press to seal the edges of the pie dough so the top and bottom crusts stick to each other, then carefully roll the crust over itself so that the rolled edge sits on the "lip" of the pie plate. Crimp the edges. Beat the reserved egg and gently brush onto the edges and top of the pie. Be careful not to drag any of the filling onto the crust because it will burn. Sprinkle the top with the sugar. Place the pie in the fridge for 20 minutes to allow the pastry to set.

Meanwhile, preheat the oven to 425°F. Line a rimmed baking sheet with foil.

Place the pie on the baking sheet and bake for 20 minutes. Reduce the oven temperature to 375°F and bake until the crust is golden brown, 30 minutes longer. Cover the edges of the crust with foil if it is browning too quickly. Let cool on a wire rack for 1 to 2 hours. Leftovers will keep at room temperature for 2 days or in the fridge for 3 days.

LOVE AND PIE

Many people have tried to learn my grandmother's recipe and many people have failed, with blackberry stains on the ceiling to prove it. Grandma makes bread dough without a measuring cup in sight and cooks without timers. When she made a blackberry pie at my house, I thought it was my perfect opportunity to watch and replicate her blackberry pie.

Since Grandpa's retirement, Grandma has taught him the culinary ropes of making roux, smothering okra, and slow-roasting a rump. He is the butter to her bread, and they are adorable to watch in the kitchen together. *So* adorable in fact that before I know it, I have missed the first steps in making the pie. Grandma has already begun simmering the berries in their own juices. The sweet voice of my grandmother apologizing for using up all my cornstarch breaks the trance of watching them work together. I smile politely and tell her to use whatever she needs, and she happily returns to her pot of berries. "See how thick it gets," she says to me while lifting her spoon with the black mash clinging to it for dear life, "That's when you know it's ready."

The next step: pie dough. It's Grandpa's job to knead the dough until Grandma declares it done. I watch both of them roll out the dough and agree on the thickness. Grandma places the dough into the pie plate, repairing any tears with her fingertips. She looks up at me and says, "It's not the kind of pie that matters if it looks perfect."

Then comes the lattice topping. This is the only time that Grandma and Grandpa have a difference of opinion. Just as he is finishing the lattice on the second pie, Grandma looks over her shoulder. "No, no, that's too much dough on top," she sweetly states. He turns around and looks straight at me, "I like the crust the best. It's my favorite part. But Grandma likes the filling." I watch him sit down at the kitchen island, calmly sipping his black coffee, while watching Grandma take off the extra pieces of latticework. Suddenly, I notice that the first of the two pies is already in the oven, baking away with "too much" dough. Everyone is happy with the pies, the filling lovers and the crust eaters. I never got her recipe, but this one's my own. And don't worry if it doesn't turn out looking perfect. It's not the kind of pie that minds such things.

BACON-LATTICED APPLE PIE

Makes one 9-inch pie (12 servings)

This pie is both sweet and salty, which is my favorite dessert combination. As the fat renders from the bacon, it begins permeating the crust of the pie with its smoky drippings. The smoky bacon, mingling with the spiced apples and bourbon-infused crust, is heavenly.

For the pie dough:

1¼ cups all-purpose flour, plus more for dusting

½ teaspoon kosher salt

1½ tablespoons granulated sugar

8 tablespoons (1 stick) cold unsalted butter, cubed

1 tablespoon bourbon (see Tip, page 241)

½ cup ice water

For the filling:

5 medium apples, peeled and thinly sliced

Juice of ½ lemon

¾ cup packed brown sugar

¼ cup granulated sugar

2 tablespoons cornstarch

1 tablespoon ground cinnamon

Pinch of freshly grated nutmeg

For assembly:

6 slices bacon

1 egg, beaten

MAKE THE PIE DOUGH:

In a stand mixer fitted with the flat beater attachment, combine the flour, salt, and sugar with your fingertips. Add the cold butter and mix on low until the dough looks like coarse sand. Turn the machine off and blend any large pieces of butter with your fingertips, making sure there are no pieces of butter larger than the size of a pea.

In a measuring cup, combine the bourbon and ice water. With the stand mixer on low, slowly dribble in the bourbon water 1 tablespoon at a time. Add just enough liquid for the dough to pull away from the sides of the bowl. (You may not need to use all the bourbon water.) Pinch the dough between your fingertips; it should be smooth, not sticky or crumbly. Gently press the dough together and shape into a disk. Wrap the disk in plastic wrap and refrigerate for at least 30 minutes or up to 3 days.

MAKE THE FILLING:

In a bowl, combine the apples, lemon juice, brown sugar, granulated sugar, cornstarch, cinnamon, and nutmeg. Toss with your fingertips until the apple slices are coated evenly.

ASSEMBLE AND BAKE THE PIE:

On a lightly floured surface, roll out the dough, rotating it in quarter-turns, until 12 to 14 inches in diameter and ⅛ inch thick. Gently fit the dough into a 9-inch pie plate.

(continued on page 241)

Trim the edges of the dough with scissors, making sure to leave at least a 1-inch overhang.

Crack the egg into a small dish. Without breaking the yolk, use a pastry brush to gently coat the bottom and sides of the pie shell with a thin layer of the egg white (reserve the remaining egg). The egg white creates a barrier between the filling and the crust as it bakes, keeping the crust from getting soggy. Refrigerate for 30 minutes.

Spoon the filling into the chilled pie shell. Place 3 bacon slices on top of the filling horizontally. Then, one by one, place the remaining 3 strips vertically, lifting every other horizontal strip to create a basket weave lattice. Crimp the edges by folding the excess overhang inward at a slight angle and pressing down firmly with your thumb. Continue crimping the edges all the way around the pie, tucking in the ends of the bacon slices as you crimp the edges. Beat the reserved egg and gently brush onto the exposed edges of the pie dough. Refrigerate the pie for 20 minutes to allow the pastry to set.

Preheat the oven to 425°F. Line a rimmed baking sheet with foil.

Place the pie on the lined baking sheet and bake for 20 minutes. Reduce the oven temperature to 375°F and bake until the crust is golden brown and the bacon is crisp, about 30 minutes. Cover the edges of the crust with foil if it is browning too quickly. Drain off any excess liquid by tipping the pie to one side. Let cool for 1 hour before serving.

Tip: Adding bourbon to pie dough may seem peculiar, but it works wonderfully—much better than water. When you add water to pie dough, the proteins in the flour are hydrated to form gluten, which makes the dough difficult to roll out and makes the crust tough. Alcohol inhibits gluten formation, which results in a consistent, tender, flaky crust that is easy to roll out every single time. And the aroma of bourbon as you roll this pie dough is heavenly! For those of you who worry your pies will taste like bourbon, don't. The alcohol evaporates during baking. If you don't have bourbon you can substitute with vodka.

PERFECT PEACH PIE

Makes one 9-inch pie

I believe the flavors used in this pie complement a perfectly ripe peach instead of over-powering its beautiful flavor. It's subtly spiced with cinnamon and vanilla seeds, and delicately infused with lemon zest. To me, it's a perfect combination. Also, I love leaving the peach wedges unpeeled since there's lots of flavor in the skin of the peach.

For the pie dough:

2½ cups all-purpose flour, plus more for dusting

1 teaspoon kosher salt

3 tablespoons sugar

2 sticks (8 ounces) cold unsalted butter, cubed

2 tablespoons bourbon (see Tip, page 241)

1 cup ice water

For the filling:

⅓ cup sugar

1 teaspoon grated lemon zest

½ teaspoon ground cinnamon

Seeds of 1 vanilla bean

1 pound unpeeled peach wedges (from about 4 peaches)

Pinch of sea salt

1 heaping tablespoon cornstarch

(continued on page 245)

MAKE THE PIE DOUGH:

In a stand mixer fitted with the flat beater attachment, combine the flour, salt, and sugar with your fingertips. Add the cold butter and mix on low until the dough looks like coarse sand. Turn the machine off and blend any large pieces of butter with your fingertips, making sure there are no pieces of butter larger than the size of a pea.

In a measuring cup, combine the bourbon and ice water. With the stand mixer on a low speed, slowly dribble in the bourbon water 1 tablespoon at a time. Add just enough liquid for the dough to pull away from the sides of the bowl. (You may not need to use all the bourbon water in the dough.) Pinch the dough between your fingertips; it should be smooth, not sticky or crumbly. Gently press the dough together. Divide in half and shape each half into a disk. Wrap each disk in plastic wrap and refrigerate for at least 30 minutes or up to 3 days.

MAKE THE FILLING:

In a large bowl, combine the sugar, lemon zest, cinnamon, and vanilla seeds and rub between your fingers to combine (this infuses the sugar). Add the peaches, sea salt, and cornstarch. Toss until the peaches are evenly coated.

For assembly:

1 egg, for brushing

1 tablespoon unsalted butter, cubed

Sugar, for sprinkling

ASSEMBLE AND BAKE THE PIE:

On a lightly floured surface, roll out 1 disk of dough, rotating it in quarter-turns, until 12 to 14 inches in diameter and ⅛ inch thick. Gently fit the dough into a 9-inch pie plate. Trim the edges of the dough with scissors, making sure to leave at least a 1-inch overhang.

Crack the egg into a small dish. Without breaking the yolk, use a pastry brush to gently coat the bottom and sides of the pie shell with a thin layer of the egg white (reserve the remaining egg for brushing the top of the pie). The egg white creates a barrier between the filling and the crust as it bakes, keeping the crust from getting soggy. (Reserve the rest of the egg for brushing the top crust.) Place in the fridge for 30 minutes.

Meanwhile, roll out the remaining disk of dough, rotating it in quarter-turns, to a ⅛-inch thickness. Cut the dough into six 1½-inch-wide strips. Place the strips on a baking sheet and set aside in the fridge until ready to assemble.

Tumble the peaches into the chilled pie shell. Scatter the butter over the peaches. Place 3 strips of dough on top of the peaches horizontally. Then, one by one, place the remaining 3 strips vertically, lifting every other horizontal strip to create a basket weave lattice. Trim the edges with scissors even with the bottom crust. Gently press to seal the edges of the pie dough so the top and bottom crusts stick to each other, then carefully roll the crust over itself so that the rolled edge sits on the "lip" of the pie plate. Crimp the edges. Beat the reserved egg and gently brush onto the edges and top of the pie. Sprinkle the top with sugar. Place the pie in the fridge for 20 minutes to allow the pastry to set.

Preheat the oven to 425°F. Line a rimmed baking sheet with foil.

Place the pie on the lined baking sheet and bake for 20 minutes. Reduce the oven temperature to 375°F, and bake until the crust is golden brown, about 30 minutes. Cover the edges of the crust with foil if it is browning too quickly. Let cool on a wire rack for 1 hour, if you can wait! Leftovers will keep at room temperature for 2 days or in the fridge for 3 days.

ACKNOWLEDGMENTS

First and foremost, to my husband and best friend, Michael. For being a constant tower of strength and support, and for creating a home that is filled with laughter, beautiful music, and lovely meals. This book is as much yours as it is mine. I love you.

To my Nashville family, you are legends. Thank you for being supportive and for being the best taste testers. Thank you for standing next to me, unfailing in love and encouragement. I love y'all.

To Dr. Jennifer Speights-Binet, for allowing me to pursue a thesis that seemed a little out of the ordinary, for seeing a spark in me I didn't know existed.

To Brooke Bell, for encouraging me over the years and gently nudging me to start my own site. It all began with you and me and a cup of coffee in Birmingham.

To Paige Doscher, for falling in love with these stories and recipes. I don't know if this book would have ever seen the light of day otherwise.

To Janis Donnaud, thank you for believing in me, for seeing the gold in people. You are a treasure.

To Tricia Levi, thank you, dear, for your encouragement and detailed attention to this project, and for being the first person to officially cook from this book!

To the HarperCollins team, you are a blessing to work with, especially Liz Sullivan, my editor, who has guided me with kindness throughout this whole process.

To my whole family, for surrounding me with love, food, and beautiful memories. This is for you.

INDEX

(Page references in *italics* refer to illustrations.)